HOWLING

LIKE WOLVES FROM

LONGWOOD DRIVE

CHICAGO TEENAGERS
IN THE
GREAT DEPRESSION

JAMES CUNNINGHAM

TRAFFORD
PUBLISHING™

 www.trafford.com

North America & international
toll-free: 1 888 232 4444 (USA & Canada)
phone: 250 383 6864 ♦ fax: 812 355 4082

JAMES CUNNINGHAM (Jim)

Howling like Wolves
from Longwood Drive

Jim Cunningham had been involved in education for 50 years in six states and one foreign country. He fulfilled the various roles of *teacher, counselor, administrator, and psychologist.* Eighteen of those years were as a member of a Catholic Religious Order, *the Christian Brothers.*

He holds a B.S. from the *University of Illinois* with a major in *Zoology,* minors in *Math* and *Physics*; a year in *De Paul University Law School,* Chicago; an M.A. in the Teaching of *English* from *St. Mary's University,* Winona, Minnesota; a Master Counselor license from the State of Illinois; and an A.B.D. (All But Dissertation) in *Counseling Psychology* at *Ohio University,* Athens, Ohio. He also attended educational summer programs in Greece and England.

Jim wrote a dissertation on English as a Second Language in 1959, (a pioneer work in the E.S.L field), while teaching at *St. Michael's High School* in Santa Fe, New Mexico. He has facilitated workshops in classroom management that have given new life to several educators.

He continues to reside in Coos Bay, Oregon for the last 26 years and has *co-facilitated Domestic Abuse Groups* and *Cancer Groups* the last five years.

Dedicated to:
My two brothers, Frank and John
and two sisters, Ciline and Nancy
who put up with me during our growing years;

And to my wife, Karen,
who supported me emotionally,
and her friend Vicki
who helped with technical computer skills.

CONTENTS

INTRODUCTION

Tom Brokaw's book, "The Greatest Generation" has led me to relate how the generation he extolled developed in our great city of Chicago; how we entertained ourselves; the kind of risks we took; how we solved problems during the period of World War II from1941-45. America was also recovering from the Great Depression, the hardships faced by the youth of that era, and the activities in which they were involved, legal or illegal, are the focus of this book.

Two of our crowd, each 21 years old, were quickly drafted, serving either in the Pacific against the Japanese, or in Europe against the Nazis. Others were drafted as they reached 18, though some volunteered. The daily news about the war revealed the fearful reality they were soon to face.

In 1943, as World War II heated up, the teenagers from the three contiguous communities on the far southwest side of Chicago (Morgan Park, Beverly Hills, and Mount Greenwood), would meet on weekend nights at Vanderpool Grade School on

95th Street, a block from the suburban Rock Island train, to share stories, generally about the war.

Friendships formed during those nights overcame the religious and economic barriers of the different communities (Beverly Hills, an affluent area with spacious homes of well-educated professionals; Morgan Park, average homes of the middle class; and Mount Greenwood, a struggling community with considerable poverty.

Those of us who had attended Catholic Grade Schools, educated to believe only Catholics were going to heaven, came to the realization that we had been living in a private world, culturally isolated from anything non-Catholic, and concluded our non-Catholic friends were as important to God as we were.

As a change of pace from the topic of the war the high risk guys would spontaneously promote some activity, often dangerous, the more dangerous the more appealing. Needless to say, we did create problems for the police, although we weren't into trashing or destroying. Jack, one of our high risk group, stated, "What do we have to lose? We could die being dangerous out on the streets here, or we could die in the war. At least here we'll have fun!"

Today many would consider our early living conditions austere. Our parents had decided to use any available money to give all five of us a Catholic school education at St. Barnabas grade school in Beverly Hills, followed by a Catholic high school education. In 1945 Dad bought a house in Beverly at 108th Street on Western Avenue.

The families of Beverly and Morgan Park did not appear to struggle like those in Mount Greenwood. They still had pleasant homes, but Dad mentioned some of their hardships:

unemployment, bills unpaid, utilities used sparingly (one light on at night in some houses); household temperatures kept low.

Mount Greenwood families suffered the most. In the western part, where our family lived, grandpa and his carpenter friends moved a small building, the size of a one car garage, from the middle of the property to 10431 South Homan Avenue, and added a piece on the front and one on the back to give the appearance of a house. A basement was added after eight years, and dormers a few years later. Several nearby families lacking money, lived in partially finished houses, and two houses remained just basements when money ran out. Loans were almost impossible to obtain.

Not many families, including our own, possessed a vehicle. To use our home phone we had to insert a nickel into the phone box similar to using a phone on the street. Refrigerators were scarce (we did have an ice box); clothes were washed by hand and hung out to dry, and dishes were washed by hand. We purchased milk from a lady a block away who milked her own cow. The community's 'pop & mom" grocery store (malls did not exist), three-fourths of a mile away, gave credit to so many that the couple owning the store went bankrupt.

Our house sat on an acre of land, on which we organized and controlled sports. The back half acre was for football and softball/baseball; the quarter acre next to the house became our hockey rink. My brothers and I, were always out-of-doors involved in sports, or finding work to add to the family budget.

The Chicago winters required two pairs of corduroy pants, one to wear to school for the week while the other was in the wash, high-top shoes like soldiers wear, or galoshes, long underwear, and a heavy jacket and gloves, plus a stocking cap.

We never thought we were poor. How could we? We never

lacked for food, had plenty of milk each day, and had our acre of land. Unemployment was common, but Father had a job and Mother could provide meals equal to those of a good chef.

My older brother and those his age were drafted a short time before the war ended, but the draft continued for a while. The fear of conflict with Russia appeared on the horizon. Being the youngest, I had been thinking of volunteering, but my brother sent me a letter from Shanghai, "Don't volunteer!" In early May1945 the Germans surrendered, and in August the Japanese surrendered.

The Depression unknowingly prepared our generation to endure and adapt to the kind of hardships we would face in the war to end all wars. We had learned that everything was possible, and never learned when to quit or how to give up.

JIM'S LIFE

Acceptance into the Christian Brothers brought direction and discipline to my life, and thus my authority and anger problems could be kept under control, and the idealism acquired from home could be maintained.

It was the eight missionary years in Nicaragua that opened my soul to the service of the disenfranchised, teaching 4th grade with 75 boys, ranging in age from 9 to 22. These years were truly life-changing years, so much poverty, so much sickness, so much hunger, and crude living conditions often with dirt floors. I recognized that teaching these students had to extend beyond teaching subject matter, to their out of school lives.

Looking down on the school's muddy fields, I commented, "This school needs a gymnasium," and I began to solicit funds from relatives and friends in Chicago. Within a year enough money came in to purchase a pre-fabricated gym (100 ft x 85 ft) from New Orleans. With the gymnasium athletic leagues of basketball and volleyball were added to baseball. Some 400 students from any and all schools, public or religious were involved, and I had opened up to the early days of ecumenism.

I have been involved in education 50 years (18 with the Christian Brothers), starting in 1951 in Indiana and Missouri, and have held positions as a teacher, counselor, administrator, and the last 25 years as a psychologist; teaching 20 subjects in grade school and 15 subjects in high schools; psychology classes in 3 different community colleges, and one graduate counseling class at Oregon State University.

Born and raised in Chicago during the Great Depression and WW II in a family of 3 boys and 2 girls, to loving parents who sacrificed to assure all of us had the opportunity to attend Catholic grade schools, high schools and colleges.

My education has been diversified because I am a life-time learner; attending classes in 16 colleges and universities in six states and two foreign countries, Greece and England. In 1945 at 16, I matriculated in St. Mary's University in Winona, Minnesota where I played first team football and basketball, making the all-league team in basketball).

In 1949 I received a BA from the U. of Illinois (major in Zoology and minors in Math and Physics). A year in De Paul Law School kept me busy before joining the Brothers. A few years later I earned an MA at St. Mary's in Teaching of English; attended the intensive Spanish program at St. Michael's U. in Santa Fe; earned a Master Counselor's license in Illinois, and finished the Doctoral classes in Psychology at Ohio University (Athens, Ohio), though not writing a thesis (called an ABD, all but dissertation). At the same time I was hired as the Director of the largest Residence Hall with 515 students. Following I was granted an Illinois license in Educational Psychology.

At 71 years old I began to write, authoring a first book entitled "Education on the Wild Side," (listed on Amazon), about the years in Nicaragua. I have a 2nd book being published, with a 3rd almost finished.

Retired the last 14 years have given me time to be president of the Hospice Board, President of our public library, 5 years facilitating Domestic Abuse groups, and visiting the dying. The last 10 years I've facilitated Cancer Support Groups, one locally and another 35 miles inland, and experienced the deaths of 23 friends. I've been facilitating 2 transitional groups every Saturday in Shutter Creek Correctional Facility (prison) at the request of the chaplain; I'm on the Board of Alternative Educational Programs and had been on the Board of the Democratic Party. Writing is a passion for me.

I have been arrested twice when helping my black brothers find jobs; and when driving a yellow cab as the only white out of a black garage on the west side of Chicago in the summer between school years. Racism still lives, even with the police.

My wife Karen and I have been 'house parents' to six teenagers at a time coming out of prison in Illinois, and we have taken into our home at least 15 troubled adults; though at 75 years of age I promised her I wouldn't bring home any more strangers, but I broke that promise twice already, with her passive approval.

1

MINI-FARM-HOME

The year was 1930 during the height of the Great Depression when our Father found an acre of land to locate his family, but he lacked money. He mentioned this to his father, "Dad, I've found an acre of land I like, but I don't have the money right now."

"I'll loan you the money." He was careful to call it a loan rather than a gift, knowing his son's Irish pride wouldn't accept charity. The acre was purchased along with a small building situated in the middle, not much larger than a one-car-garage.

Grandpa hired carpenter-friends to move the building forward to the muddy street at 10431 S. Homan Avenue, and to place additions to the front and back of the structure to make it resemble a house.

Meanwhile Mother had been enjoying her life living near her parents and 8 other siblings in St. Columbanus Parish. She said to Dad, "Here we have plenty of family, my parents, my brothers and sisters; and your sister's family is only a few blocks away. All of them help me care for our boys when you are on the road."

Beginning of Porch for House. Dad with his five children

"But, I've already purchased the land and the house!"

Mom clarified one serious concern, "You and your dad are going to install indoor plumbing before we move in, aren't you?" Mother had a premonition that in this rural area some houses did not have indoor plumbing, and she was right.

"Have you forgotten my father's a master plumber, and I still have a plumber's license?"

Father wanted his boys to feel the freedom to roam the prairies, reminding Mother, "The Irish came from peasant stock, and have a love of the land." However, he hadn't foreseen a special benefit for his sons. The prairies were composed of rolling mounds, and in the winter what joy his sons would have ice skating for miles on the ice-covered water in the low areas between the mounds.

Then there was the half-acre on the back street dedicated to football and softball/baseball. Beside the house father helped us bank the sides of the property to create our own hockey rink. The lack of sport paraphernalia did not deter us; our creative talents were put to use for this and any other activities. Actually we didn't have any other choice.

In the 30's FDR created the WPA (named by us as 'We Play Always'), a part of his New Deal. The workers were installing a five foot diameter sewer system down our street, in front of our house. Some of the workers would let us kids use their shovels to work for them, while they rested and got warm inside our four foot diameter hollowed out tree, three workers at a time. Of course we saw our work as fun.

Although a city boy, father began to bring home all sorts of animals. The favorite was our female goat, Topsie. We would take her off her chain (she'd eat rope) to play football with us, and she would run with it in her mouth while we tried to tackle her. She had her own residence, built like a doghouse, filled with straw. During some severe Chicago winters we placed her in a neighbor's cow barn for warmth.

The fun was to buck with her, and not get hurt. She loved the competition, especially when she could get up on her hind legs to add force, but that was the time to move out of the way!

When my older brother, Frank, left for the Navy, and I entered college, dad gave Topsie to a goat farm, where she died. The truth of her death was revealed later by the farmer, "She died of homesickness. She wouldn't eat and wouldn't mix with the other goats. She missed the boys, and just dwindled away."

Dad increased the number of our dogs to six, including two racing dogs, Pic and Pat, followed by several cats that kept multiplying. Our chickens and ducks had their own coop with an abundance of space surrounded by wire fencing. Rats, living in the woodpile out back, were large, at least half the size of a cat, and sufficient in number to serve the meat needs of our cats and dogs. Mother directed us, "Only feed the cats milk, and they will remain excellent hunters."

Each month, Mary, the lady next door, would show up with a large turtle she caught. After killing it she'd hang it upside down from her clothesline to let the blood drain out into a pan on the ground for soup. She had the reputation of being the creator of excellent soups, enriched with wild plants she collected from the neighboring prairies. Once Mary asked us, "Do you want a taste?"

I answered, "Mother wouldn't approve" However, the truth was: "We didn't want to drink blood."

The Naughton family, neighbors on the back street, had a large black male German Shepherd dog in their fenced-in yard, and they warned us, "Don't come over the fence into our yard when we're not there. Our dog is dangerous."

My favorite cat, a beautiful female with a gray coat, a white belly and white boots, was a superb hunter. During a battle she won with one of the larger rats, she experienced a serious wound that required a month of care to heal. She could not be kept out of the house: She would open a dormer window from the roof, or she'd crawl along the pipes under the house to the trap door leading to the bathtub plumbing, and push it open, determined to sleep on the fold-out couch with Frank and me.

The story about my cat and this large dog I used for an oral presentation in a high school English class. "I know it will be difficult to believe, but I watched it in amazement. That dangerous dog escaped his yard, entered our yard, and began growling when he sighted our dog Butch. All fluffy white, not much larger than the cat, Butch tried to move closer to Kitty, asleep on the back stairs sunning herself.

The relationship of Kitty and Butch needs to be told in order to understand what followed. They had grown up together and had become life-long buddies. Every day they played, generally boxing. Kitty would stand on her two back legs and bop Butch with her front paws, left, right, left, right, without extending her claws. In frustration, he would try to overcome her, initially attacking head first, but her boxing technique impeded his vision. Then he would turn his butt toward her to push her down, and they'd start all over again. Kitty, always in control, would be careful not to hurt him.

She awakened when she heard the growling, recognized that her playmate was in trouble, shot off the stairs as though propelled by some invisible force, and with long quick strides landed on the German shepherds back, directly behind his head, viciously clawing at his face. Yelping, he ran off with Kitty still clawing. Finally she jumped off and returned to rub against Butch, a sign of her affection, and positioned herself back on the stairs.

It was a sad day for me when, after fifteen years of life, she died. I gently placed her in a marked grave under one of the flowering bushes in the yard, a cross on top, and said a prayer, "Please God, put her where I can see her again."

Another neighbor a block down the street, Mrs. Colhon, an immigrant from Eastern Europe, owned five acres she would seed with hay and alfalfa each year to feed her cow. Early most mornings my two brothers and I would run down to her barn to be there when she milked, and at times she'd say, "Here's a shot of milk," as she squirted the selected one as he tried to catch the milk in his mouth. She would pour the milk into a bucket through a clean cloth made from a sugar sack. Her cow could fill a pail in the morning and another in the evening. The milk, so rich, that after a year four of us developed boils. Mother decided to change to the milkman who rode by each morning on his horse-drawn wagon, and leave a six quart-rack of milk-bottles on the back porch.

After 10 yrs, house with basement, but lacking dormers upstairs

CHAPTER

2

MOTHER'S STORY

Two years after reluctantly moving to the remote property Dad had purchased, mother related a portion of her family's history to her three sons.

"My parents came from a small farm town in Missouri, Milan by name, and their ancestors, the O'Donnell clan (known in western Ireland for piracy) and the Ryan clan, can be traced for several generations back to the 'Old Sod.' The O'Donnell Clan migrated to Chicago by way of Quincy, Illinois, but most of the Ryan Clan remained on their farms in Missouri. My younger sister Eileen and I came late to our family of nine children; we blossomed from the extra love of the older ones: Ethel, Michael, Charlie, Harry, Leo, Margie, and Eva. They spoiled us and spoiled you three boys. You were born so fast, one each year, and for a brief time all three of you were in cloth diapers at the same time. You were a handful for me. Only twenty-one, I don't know how I could have handled you boys in your baby years without the help of my family!"

Mother had become a good cook early on, learning well at

the side of her mother and three older sisters. The repetitive plan of her meals remains imbedded in my memory. After Mass on Sunday, breakfast consisted of one egg, two sausage links, and hot cereal with milk. All other mornings it was hot oatmeal or cream of wheat, and plenty of milk. Sunday dinner would be a roast, potatoes, a vegetable, rice pudding or bread pudding for dessert, and always milk. Leftovers had to last for the next three days, and she would put together whatever existed in the house for the other three days. Mother's words, "Remember we all belong to the clean plate club," were meant as a gentle reminder during those hard times. There could never be leftovers on our plates.

Dad would have made the same point in a forceful voice, "Anything you put on your plate you will eat."

Every so often Mother would expand her personal story. With three boys in diapers, she spent some part of each day washing those smelly articles by hand, and after a year she finally mentioned the need for a wringer washer to dad, "Frank, I need a wringer washer and some place where it can be used."

I'm sure dad had been thinking about mother's burden since his answer provided an immediate solution. "I can dig out a ten foot square space under the house with a trench to reach it from the furnace area" (Since a basement didn't exist, 'trench' meant as in war).

Mother's appreciation would be proclaimed to her family and neighbors, "With the help of Frankie and Jimmie, not more than six and five years old, I could hang up the wet clothes on a rope-line outside, even in our Chicago winters. They were also responsible for the dirty dishes."

Some years later, Mother reminisced with friends, "During the early months Frank was 'on the road', I cared for the boys and all the animals. We had no car, and TV didn't exist, so I had only a pay telephone in which a nickel had to be inserted each time, if I had a nickel. The phone was like any pay-phone out on a street corner. When nickels weren't available I used slugs, and when the phone man came each month to collect the coins, he would separate the slugs and claim cash for them. A nickel-phone was a luxury since that was the cost of any call irrespective of time. The cost of our neighbors' phone-calls was based on time, thus frequently a lady neighbor would ask Mother to use our phone for a more lengthy call."

John, the youngest, recalled the fun times we had shopping, "When mother was only twenty one, she would promenade with us to the only grocery store in the neighborhood, three-fourths of a mile away. Our walks would be festive events as we skipped along, singing songs mother had taught us. As soon as we were in the store, we would rush around looking at everything, touching what we shouldn't, ending at the candy counter."

We would stand there, faces pressed against the glass, pleading with mother, "Mother, can't we have some candy?" At times she couldn't resist, bought candy, and returned home without purchasing much. She did have a charge account similar to what can be seen in 'Little House on the Prairie,' but she wouldn't use it except in emergencies. She had to be frugal and would choose food judiciously since she lacked a refrigerator.

On these occasions Mother would ask the butcher, "Do you have a soup bone I could have, and maybe some liver?" People didn't consider a bone or liver eatable, but she could make a healthy meal out of anything, especially something free.

Three brothers (John, Frank, and Jim) on sidewalk poured by Father in front of house in Mount Greenwood (1932)

Raising three little boys and living in their world dictated how mother viewed life. Added to the owner of the store and a few infrequent neighbors, Mothers' other adult contacts were the seasonal door-to-door salesmen with their small talk. These motley-looking men were numerous: a knife sharpener pushing his musical contraption; the once a year organ grinder with music and a monkey; a salesman selling shoestrings and knickknacks from a suitcase at a nickel or dime; another, marketing twenty pound bags of coal from his horse and wagon; and a 'hawker' with horse and wagon, wanting to buy 'rags and old iron.' Mother lived in this one-of-a-kind world, finding ways to handle any hardship, and convert it into fun.

When we were older, I said to her, "Mother, you were always compassionate. You could never turn anyone away without buying something, something that might cost your last coin."

Now-a-days who could imagine a small woman like her, barely five feet tall, with three little boys, opening her door to unknown merchants? She never locked the door, even at night; trusting people was an integral part of her being.

Our younger sister, Nancy, revealed the real reason no door was locked, "Mother lost the key."

Looking back to our early years we admitted, "Mother's hardships were comparable to women of the old Wild West."

About the use of the house by her boys, she would say, "I don't want anything that would restrict the play of my sons." The house became our playground in bad weather. Our favorite activity was to do flips from the iron bed frame onto the mattress. Mother took delight in watching the flips, and being sure no one would be injured.

Within the next four years two girls were born. Managing three boys and two diapered little girls, Mother said to dad, "Frank, I need help controlling Jim and Frank. They are getting wild." With our bicycles we could reach areas several miles from home in any direction, and mother had no idea where we were.

"I can take charge of them if that would be helpful."

Mother showed relief with a deep sigh, and a "Yes."

She was to keep track of our misdeeds, and relate them to Dad when he returned home on weekends. If they agreed the misbehaviors were serious enough, Dad would walk Frankie and me into the bedroom, lock the door, take out his belt, and have us bend over the bed, Frankie first. The beatings did not reduce our wildness; in fact, we stated, "We were born to be wild!"

Dad's form of punishment lasted longer than mother could endure, and each time she'd bang on the door, shouting, "That's enough, Frank! "That's enough!"

The beatings tended to be cruel. Returning home Friday nights after being on the road in Indiana and Michigan, Dad was overly tired, so he tended to be excessive. Each time it seemed as though he was trying to be forceful enough to end any need to repeat the ordeal. What is sad is he cared about us, but was limiting positive father-son relationships. So many fathers in those days were physical with their sons, with the belief they had to be disciplined.

Within a year Mother assumed total control of any punishments Frank and I received, selecting her washing 'tools' to do the job: a large wooden spoon to pull hot clothes from the wringer, and a three foot long broom handle used to stir the clothes. The wooden spoon became her primary discipline weapon. Later I 'fessed up' "We three brothers would make the wooden spoons disappear by going up into the attic and dropping them down the inside wall. Thinking she had lost the previous one, in time she would buy another."

During one of our teenage evening gatherings with the guys, Frank mentioned, "The worst beating we ever received however, came from Mother and her three foot long broom handle. Following the removal of our clothes to be washed, Mother became enraged, and beat us on the back of our bare legs with such force we had welts for a month.

"Why would your mother beat you like that?"

"She was scared we could die."

"I don't understand," Mickie replied.

"We had gone swimming in the sand dunes at 103rd and California. A few months previously a neighbor youth swimming there came down with sleeping sickness and died."

"How did she find out?"

"We neglected to shake the sand from our clothes."

In 1938, Grandpa John died, leaving enough inheritance to put in a basement. The house was raised mostly with men's muscles, large heavy-duty jacks, and 12 x 12 inch beams. We three boys and the older of our two younger sisters were sent to a camp for two weeks (Nancy, the youngest, went to an aunt's), while the cement basement became a reality. No longer did Mother need to walk through a damp trench to wash clothes.

Talking about the construction of the basement Frankie reminded me of the trip to obtain medicine he and I made, "Do you recall that time when Mother became very sick from being down in that cold damp trench too often, and you and I, nine and ten years old, walked five miles round trip to the Beverly pharmacy in a Chicago winter storm to get her some medicine?" There was no limit to what we would do for mother and so we considered this task like any other task, though we nearly froze to death.

Every summer Dad would obtain train passes for all of us to travel to Quincy, Illinois, where we lived for two weeks in our maternal grandmother's converted barn behind her rented-out house. Visiting the great Mississippi River and roller skating on well paved sidewalks were our joys. Then we continued to Milan, Missouri, to live on farms with our cousins. In Milan mother and dad and our two sisters would stay in town with mom's cousin, Molly Moffet, while we three boys went to the farms where we could ride horses with cousins. Mother would spend most of her time with a group of women weaving patched quilts, while Dad found a haven in the town square every day sitting with the farmers, listening to their stories, and asking questions once in a while. It was obvious that he could relax with these men who enjoyed an uncomplicated life.

On the farms, my brothers and I found an abundance of food, plenty of milk from the herd of cows, and a lot of homemade ice cream. We learned that when getting up in the middle of the night to piss we could do so through the screen window from the second floor, and due to the heat we also learned to sleep in the raw.

We rode their horses bareback, even though we had no previous experience with them. However, we found equal entertainment riding the huge pigs. We would hop on those pigs, and run them around the barn yard, as they squealed as if being slaughtered. Another entertaining game was corncob wars. A corncob itself couldn't hurt much, but when caked with dried manure and aimed well, it could put an adversary down for the count. Our cousins, about our ages, weren't quite up to the rough play of their city relatives.

Aware of the financial plight of the Ryans, Dad would quietly contribute cash to the three families that hosted us.

3

FATHER'S WAYS

This chapter is entitled Father's Way because he worked out-of-state Monday through Friday, and would be in charge only on weekends. Nevertheless he managed all the problems Frank and I would cause, and with his influential friends in the Democratic Party he would find solutions.

Only 5'7" and about 150 pounds, Dad was an excellent athlete, quick with his fists, quite handsome with strong features, a heavy beard and coal black hair, evidence of Spanish blood in his Irish ancestry.

After graduating from De La Salle in1924, from a Catholic High School taught by the Christian Brothers, he was recruited by a semi-pro football team in the 'rough and tumble' Chicago city league, and paid the large sum of $5 a game to serve as running back, a position he had occupied in high school.

At the same time he worked as a bouncer/usher in the Grove Theater on Cottage Grove Avenue. Every so often, on a Sunday, he would take us three boys there, enter from the back to chat with the building engineer, an old friend, and send us into the theater to watch 'Snow White.'

Dad had a variety of friends, rich and poor, important and questionable. Once on a late evening in September, around my 10th birthday, Dad and I walked the two miles through the prairies to the bar of Mike King-Tom Long on Western Avenue, a watering hole for south side Irish politicians.

He introduced me to Johnny Duffy, president of the Cook County Board. Johnny had been elected president of the Cook County Board. In my college years, during Easter vacation, I worked for Johnny in his Floral Business on Halsted Street, 20 hours each day, Thursday – Sunday, with paid time off to attend Mass. Most employees working at the Floral Shop came from Duffy's extended family, plus a few like me of Irish extraction, as a favor to Father. A large number of county and city political jobs, were allocated to the Irish. Two Catholic law schools, De Paul and Loyola, favored Catholic candidates.

Later an old friend, Matt Capone, the younger brother of Al Capone, approached Dad, greeting him with a hearty hand-shake, "Hi Frank, remember me from our years at St. Calumbanus grade school?"

"Of course Matt," (Dad had an extraordinary memory for names). "Jim, this is an old school friend of mine, Matt Capone."

During the evening, though I don't remember why, Matt took out a $5 bill. "Here's how to recognize a fake," he said, pointing to the numbers in the shadows of the bushes on the back.

On our way home, through the same prairies, Dad explained, "Al had placed his younger brother in Notre Dame University to obtain a good education, and to keep him out of his kind of

Dad with Pat, one of his greyhounds, in front of our first car, a Model A Ford, given to him by his boss. The 3 boys sat in the rumble seat, open in the summer and closed over them in the winter to keep warm.

business. However, Al didn't consider the machinations of the Chicago police. Any time Matt would be coming home in his fancy convertible, police would arrest him, and release him when Al sent over a pay off."

Dad admitted, "I was usually with Matt, but the family didn't approve."

Dad didn't mention the rumor shared by my older brother, "I heard that Mom and Dad went on their honeymoon in one of Al Capone's limousines."

When Dad decided to settle down, he bypassed his training in plumbing, and chose to work with the Eastern Weighing and Inspection Bureau at the Board of Trade on La Salle Street in downtown Chicago. His territory covered Indiana and Michigan where he inspected the movement of grain from one train system to another. One train system could cheat the other by watering down the grain before the transfer, thereby increasing the weight and the monetary value. He would find a room in a grubby two story hotel during the week and return home Friday night.

The grain and stock market, located in the Board of Trade, functioned somewhat like a gambling casino where millions could be made or lost. A few of our St Barnabas grade school classmate's fathers had seats on the Board. However, without the money to buy a seat, Dad developed friendships that could provide access to potential business opportunities, and the frequent poker games. He enjoyed the risks of poker and won most of the time.

The time away from his sons, and his concern about Mother's brothers' and sisters' involvement with us, began to bother him. He believed the growing favoritism of Mother's family was interfering with the cohesiveness he wanted for his family, what he didn't have in his growing -up years. If he were honest, he would admit to being jealous. He did share with Mother, "Your brother Mac favors Frankie; Ethel favors Jim, her godson; and Grandma has taken a shine to John."

There was a caring unselfish side to Dad that indicated how much he wanted to take pride in us. Once while buying shoes, Frankie whispered to John and me, "We're getting new shoes while Dad has cardboard in his." Another time, when I was complaining about something, Frankie reminded me of Dad's charity, "Can't you see how many of our neighbors come here to ask for help? Stop complaining."

On one occasion when our family went downtown in our Model-A Ford to observe a special event, Dad noticed a man's shadow in the dark entry of a store closed for the night. He stopped to check on this man's wellbeing. I asked my brother, "Why is he stopping at this corner (Van Buren and Wabash, a smaller skid-row area of Chicago)?"

"I don't know. It doesn't make sense!"

Dad began a one way conversation with this disheveled thirty year old man, a one way conversation because the man stuttered so badly he couldn't say his name (Joe). Dad had him get into the rumble seat with us three boys. Joe stayed with our family for two years as Dad spent time teaching him to slow down and control his breathing. After two years Joe brought his stuttering under control, and Dad bought him a train ticket that would carry him to a Catholic seminary where he was to study for the priesthood.

Father wanted us to know some of his family's history, and began to share in response to our questions. "Your grandfather arrived from Ireland around 1900, settled down in Chicago, and worked as a house boy for a priest. He soon took up plumbing, which led to the accumulation of considerable wealth." Dad revered his father, adding, "He lost much of his wealth during the Great Depression, and his wife, my mother, and your grandmother, died before all of you were born. I don't believe he's ever recovered from those losses.

Your grandfather hated the English, and in halting words gave meaning to his hatred. Quite emotional he spoke in such a strong brogue he was difficult to understand. "Under the power of the English Empire Irish peasants were starving and dying during the potato famine in the mid 1800's. Some found seaweed and other marine plants as a source of food, and would enter the dangerous waters surrounding their island late at night. When overly desperate they didn't hesitate to pick seaweed even under a bright moon, a time when English soldiers would shoot at them for target practice." To add to the cruelty of the English soldiers, grandfather stated, "My mother would recall the names of family members that the English soldiers walked over, whether those poor souls were dead or dying,"

His final words, said seriously, brought chills down our spines, "If I thought I had any English blood in me, I'd cut my veins open and let it all pour out!"

Grandpa loved Chicago, and saw it as a melting pot of ethnic enclaves, separated geographically. He belonged to this great city as though born and bred here. If he had lived a few years more, he could have trumpeted, "Look at all the Irish mayors of Chicago: Kelley, Kennelly, and the Daleys, father and son."

He had paid the boat fare from Ireland for three men, but one stands out, Willie. I'm not sure he was a relative, but Willy's hatred of the English was as extreme as grandpa's. Any objective person hearing their stories would call what was happening to the Irish as genocide.

Dad, a Democratic precinct captain in Chicago's 19th Ward, had considerable power to aid those who lived in his precinct, a fact readily understood by anyone who has had knowledge of Chicago politics. He could have the city trucks plow snow for a needy citizen, or spread gravel in someone's driveway, get a political job for a struggling father, and help with other material needs.

Father emphasized the importance of a good education, making sure each of his children had the opportunity for a college education. He would support us in any school conflicts. Only once did he need to take my side against an English teacher, Brother Eugene , who accused me of talking during a test. Standing over me he said, "You are talking during the test. Tear it up."

"You're kidding, aren't you?"

"No, I'm not. Tear it up!"

Seated in the front desk in the middle row, I looked up at him to ask a question while pointing to a line on the test. "Can you explain this phrase to me?" And for that, my test was to be torn up. Sitting there befuddled as he walked away, slowly I folded the test and placed it neatly in my pocket. I could not accept his directive. I wanted to challenge him right then in front of my classmates, but chose to hold my tongue, and remained silent, sitting there in anger. I knew Brother Eugene did not like our class, the brightest class in a homogenously grouped system, and I knew he considered me the primary trouble-maker like my older brother. (The difference between us was I was ranked 3rd among my class at our graduation.)

At home I explained the situation to Dad. An alumnus of the high school, the next morning he went with me to confer with the principal, Brother Francis, who called Brother Eugene to his office. In fairness to Brother Eugene, he did admit without hesitating, "I acted foolishly. Yes, Jim's story is correct."

The principal directed him, "Brother, please correct this error."

Since I had the partially-finished test in my pocket, I handed it to him, "Here's the test, Brother. I didn't tear it up."

The following day, in front of my classmates, Brother Eugene called me forward to say, "I want to return your test. You did well."

I wasn't surprised to receive an 'A' because I finished the test at home!

Looking up at him, I said, "Thanks much, Brother."

The few times Frank and I, together or individually, ended in jail, Dad would be there to get us out, and had a way of asking the desk sergeant for the reason we were apprehended. He had the skill to coax the police to recognize the trivial reasons for' collaring' us. Of course, he would 'throw around names' of important politicians as his friends, to influence the desk-sergeant. Dad's way would convince the sergeant of the insignificant charge and receive an apology.

Only once did Father become angry with Frank when he returned home one night. Dad grabbed him when he came in, believing he was the cause of my being in jail. Angrily Dad questioned, "What did you do to get Jim in jail?"

"Look at me, Dad! I'm in a suite! I was on a date! I wasn't with Jim!"

"Well, go with me to get him out." Inviting Frank to accompany him was Dad's way of apologizing.

Of the 25+ guys who gathered most weekend nights on a grade school property at 95th Street, most were in the 'War to End All Wars.' In order to graduate from high school, my brother was allowed to delay his entry into the Navy. He entered the Great Lakes Naval Base the day after graduation. I was too young to be drafted. I could have volunteered, and was about to, until I received a letter from Frank when stationed in Shanghai, advising me, "Don't do it!"

Dad could not protect Frankie from being drafted, but he did make an effort to protect me. He approved and paid for me to enter college at 16, later revealing to my younger brother John, "Your mother and I don't want to risk losing 2 sons." And so I learned vicariously about the horrors of war through the stories of the guys who came home, many suffering from serious injuries, and living with the unknown illness of PTSD (Post traumatic stress), not acknowledged in WW II.

After the war Dad would frequent Paul's Swiss Chalet, an

upbeat bar a block down the street, where he chatted with several of the returning vets from our group. His kindness and sympathy for the veterans led to an invitation to stop by our house at any hour, and they did, always a bit tipsy at around 2 am to sleep on a couch. However Bill Lee, always alone, came to talk with Dad.

Chicago 1941
Downtown Chicago – primarily women; men readying for war

4

BILL LEE

After the war Dad would frequent Paul's Swiss Chalet, an upbeat bar a block down the street, where he chatted with several of the returning vets from our old group. His kindness and sympathy led to an invitation to stop by our house at any hour. Only three individuals appeared, making good use of this invitation. Two guys would walk in around two or three in the morning, a bit 'tipsy' to sleep on the couch, but the third, Bill Lee, came alone to talk more with Dad.

Bill's entrance was noisy from the clatter of his impaired legs, full of shrapnel that couldn't be removed. Returning from the Pacific Theater he was admitted to a California VA hospital where the doctors wanted to remove his legs. Bill would not allow it, "I'd rather live with what I have or die trying, than have my legs cut off!"

My brother, stationed in California, visited Bill whenever possible, and when he returned home, he shared with me, "You won't believe how thin Bill is, skin and bones, 88 pounds on his 6' 6" frame. A couple of times in that hospital, when heavily drugged, he tried to cut off his own legs with the metal edge of a foot-long ruler."

Bill would stand at the bottom of the stairs to the second floor. Usually I would be the first to awaken. "Hi Bill, how ye doin?"

"I want to talk with your Dad!"

"He's upstairs. You know the way." Bill's strong arms dominated as he pulled on the banister to help his legs. Most of the muscle of one leg had been destroyed, and the primary nerve in that leg had been seriously damaged such that he couldn't move it on its own; he had to throw it forward.

Our parent's bedroom door permitted easy access; Bill would plop himself down on the side of their bed to talk for about a half hour, and return downstairs.

"Do you want to play the piano?" I asked.

"Yes!" sitting down at our baby grand piano, he'd run his huge hands up and down the keys to limber up.

"What are you going to play?"

"Some Tchaikovsky," and he did, at a volume that vibrated the piano and shook the pictures on the wall. Everybody knew Bill was visiting. After an hour he went to sleep on the couch, and the next morning had coffee and whatever with Dad.

Besides being an excellent pianist, he had played golf at a low handicap, and had become a dominant player in the Chicago 16 inch softball league. With so much athletic ability lost, one would believe he would be depressed; he was, until he looked forward to entering the University of Illinois.

Before he made the decision for a college education, Bill would be drunk most nights, frequenting one of the two cocktail lounges in the neighborhood where most of the vets gathered, and would sit quietly in their company, after which one of us would drive him home, if he would go.

By the fall of 1946, Bill had won the struggle for sobriety with the commitment to AA, wanting to be ready to enter the University. He and my brother Frank, on the G.I. Bill, made the trek together to the University of Illinois in Urbana. Since Bill's older brother Bob happened to be the secretary (the money man) of Psi Upsilon Fraternity, both pledged to that fraternity. Otherwise housing was impossible to find due to the deluge of World War II vets.

Dad wanted me to follow them, "Go to the University of Illinois with your brother and Bill Lee!"

"But, there's no housing there, and hasn't been for months."

"That's no excuse. Go door to door until someone takes the risk to have a student living with them." I had no choice when Dad talked like that. I knew what he was implying, "Get going!" So I did go door to door, easily finding a couple of old ladies willing to rent their large comfortable attic. I think my youthful appearance won them over, however Bob Lee found a slot for a new pledge. The fraternity became my home along with Bill and Frank.

Many nights, completely asleep on a top bunk, where Bill had pinned himself in, he would be screaming and shouting about the Japanese soldiers drunk on sake, coming over a 5 foot mound of dead Japanese soldiers. He was back there again, facing the vision and hearing the unending yelling, in such a manner, as Bill said, "Marines were scared shit-less." Bill also scared other fraternity members near shit-less.

Often Bill had serious foot infections, and would spend time in the university hospital. In that era the University required two years of a language to graduate, and Bill, missing so many Spanish classes, received a midterm grade of 'F.' The university counselor had carelessly placed both Bill and me in Spanish II, bypassing Spanish I. He considered our one year of high school Spanish before the War as equal to a full year of college Spanish. Neither of us could put two Spanish words together. After the first week I said, "This level is way over my head." I considered dropping out, but Jose, sitting next to me in the back row, was fluent in the language. Noticing the timidity of the teacher hiding behind her book, I asked him, "Can you help me Jose?"

"Sure. During tests I can put my paper close enough for you to copy."

In and out of the hospital, failing Spanish, I advised him, "Transfer to our class, and we'll carry you in our system." Because of his health problems, the transfer was easy, and Bill became a member of our back row. At the end of the semester all the back row members (all males) received an 'A' grade, but Bill received a 'B.' For the second semester of Spanish II, we followed Jose into the class with that same teacher of the first semester of Spanish II, and all our back row members including Bill, received an 'A' for the final.

Many people considered what we did as 'cheating.' I say, "We were in an unjust situation, and had to make an adjustment."

In his seventies Bill died, still living in the old neighborhood. Dad had died several years before him. There was something about Dad's compassion and listening skills that drew vets to him to reveal their fears of that horrible war they survived.

Their sunken eyes from lack of sleep, their wordless disposition, and staring out into space told a story of unbelievable adjustments, survival in spite of the horrors, fears so overwhelming they lost control of body functions in battle, drunk most nights, yet they were courageous, these men who survived physically, though never emotionally. Dad's way taught those of us who didn't go to that war how to understand their sufferings.

CHAPTER

5

SUMMER RECREATION

In the late hot Chicago nights of 1942-45, going for a swim would be our primary choice to get out of the heat, and we had many swimming options. (The air conditioned Beverly Theater was our final option).

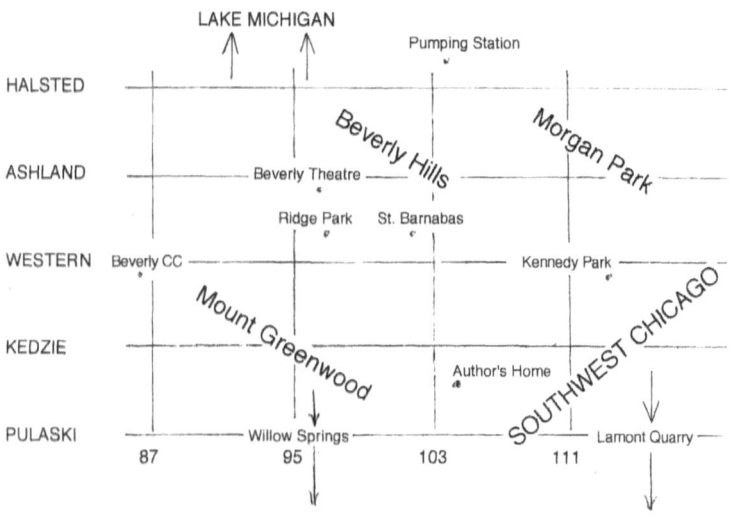

1) Kennedy Park's two outdoor pools at 113th and Western;
2) Ridge Park indoor pool at 97th and Longwood Drive;
3) Beverly Country Club at 87th and Western;
4) Mr. B's family pool on Longwood Drive
5) Hutchinson family pool in North Beverly.
6) Lamont Quarry several miles west on 111th Street
7) Pumping Station, east on 103rd Street
8) Willow Springs pool west on 95th Street

KENNEDY PARK was our usual 'hang out' in our early teens. We would sit around telling stories until 9 p.m., waiting for darkness.

My older brother, Frank, was the athlete of our group of about 20 males. I was the youngest by almost two years, yet the best diver/swimmer, and the first to say, "Let's go swimming!"

Frank would pick up the mood, "Come on guys, get off your asses and let's go for a swim." He would stay behind to help the less agile over the fence surrounding the pools.

We always chose the boys' pool, the location of the ten foot high diving board. When inside everyone stripped to his skivvies and threw their clothing aside.

A 'cannon ball' style jump from the ten foot high board attracted the larger bodies of the group, but they didn't take advantage of the spring of the diving board. That required better balance. Generally one making a canon ball would shout, "Look out below!" knowing the force of his splash could drown the others. I took advantage of the spring of the diving board to complete a one and a half front-flip or a reverse jack-knife, dives I had been doing for years.

Our swimming instructor during our younger years, a part-time professional clown, spent extra time teaching trick dives. He said to me, "You'd be an ideal clown because you're fearless."

No authority figures, including the police, ever bothered us.

RIDGE PARK, contrary to Kennedy Park, was an inside pool, somewhat more difficult to get in. A high window, usually left open to release humidity, would be our entry point, but its height and small opening required someone to be boosted up. "Jim, you're the smallest. You can do it," Pete asserted, and I was more than willing. This was the pool in which most of us had learned to swim, and we continued to respect it.

One night upon entering, we encountered a strong smell. Jack noticed its source first, ""Someone shit on the diving board!"

Kevin jokingly commented, "Whoever dumped this smelly pile must have stored it for a week." All traces of the 'evil deed' were quickly cleaned up, and deposited in the toilet located in the adjoining men's bathroom.

Taking down the canoe hung on the wall to paddle up and down the pool became one of the more desirous activities, considerable fun in spite of the short distance. The life-saving rings were used to float around, always remembering to return them and any other toys to their original location.

After an hour or two, Joe would announce, "We'll have to clean up the pool, and that means not leaving any evidence for the administration that someone had been using the facility." (Joe's dad, many years as the CEO of a large pie factory, had recently opened his own pie factory).

Before leaving Pete reminded us, "Make sure to spread the word, not to ruin a good thing. Don't trash the pool!"

The PUMPING STATION only attracted a few, probably because the Water Board established the rule: "Swimming only in the nude." Many teenage males, contrary to what some might believe, feel embarrassed running around with their equipment hanging out and bouncing around. Obviously girls had different times than boys.

BEVERLY HILLS COUNTRY CLUB ($25,000 membership in those years) maintained a large sized pool with high and low dives. Though a beautiful setting, we rarely took advantage unless someone had a car. Club members would stand on the second floor deck, and lean on the railing of their luxurious club house to watch us swim in their pool, about a football field away. Our fans enjoyed our activities, and laughed heartily. Jack commented, "They must believe we are the sons of members, or I'm sure they would be calling the police."

The WILLOW SPRINGS POOL OUT 95TH STREET, like an Olympic pool, was never one of our secretive adventures because it stayed open late into the night. However, it was exciting with various diving boards at different heights. Whenever we had enough money and someone had a car, we would drive out there, packed into that one car. It had been said that only the high-risk-divers would dare use the 25 foot board, but when we stood below all those boards I looked up and casually stated, "That highest board doesn't seem all that high."

Frank asked, "Are you going up there?"

"Why not?"

Then Jack threw out the challenge, "You won't dare dive from up there!" It was rare for Jack to challenge anyone because he was the extreme thrill seeker of our group, and would be the first one to take up the challenge.

"I sure will!" Any challenge would start my adrenaline flowing, and I had to respond, "I'll do a one and a half front-flip from up there." Further evaluation however brought to light that almost everyone stopped at the ten foot board. Only a few continued to the twenty-five foot level, and then they would only jump, not dive. I thought, "Have I opened myself to more than I can accomplish?"

After changing into our swimming togs, Jack expressed his challenge again, "Are you really going to dive from that highest board?"

"Sure, but I'll progress from the ten foot board first." When I reached the ten foot board I accomplished a one and a half front-flip; then it was up to the challenged highest board. Climbing up that ladder fifteen more feet gave me the feeling of a hundred feet. I hesitated, and unwisely looked down! I had to hang on tight as my hands began to shake and my skin felt like someone was sticking me with pins. Reaching the top, I thought seriously about turning back. Looking at the narrow board that reached out at least six feet beyond the support structure, I felt panicky. I wasn't sure I could slither out there on all fours, let alone walk out there; but a challenge had to be answered. Slowly I crept out to the end, and again looked down. Everyone in the pool appeared tiny! Another surge of fear consumed me, my heart beating like an African drum; the considerable bounce of the board, more than any other board I've ever experienced in my life. I thought, "This board could throw me up and out into the distance, so far I could reach the cement on the other side of the pool." Again I thought of crawling back! I bounced as little as possible, and went into my one and a half front-flip, performing the dive correctly, smoothly entering the water.

I bragged to the guys, "I'll do it again." Once accomplished, the second time did not provide as much fear as the first. After two good dives I was getting cocky, and impulsively decided, "I'll do a two and a half front flip this time," a dive I had always wanted to try, but never did. Erroneously I thought this extra height would provide enough time to add the extra flip. However the body tried to stop at one and a half while the mind tried to force a two and a half front flip. The conflict of body and mind, each compromising half way down, somewhere between a one and a half and two and a half, I landed on my back. Oh, did that hurt! But the rule of divers is, "Get back up and do it again before fear takes over." I proclaimed, "This second time I will do it;" but I landed on my back again. Demonstrating this degree of fearlessness, I could then say to the guys, "I think this dive will have to wait for another day." Pride saved!

Many years later, watching the Olympic Diving Trials on TV, I said out loud, more to self, "The high levels are stable platforms, not spring boards!"

THE LAMONT QUARRY, several miles west on 111th Street, required hitchhiking to get there. The distance motivated us to carry something to eat because we generally stayed all day, always on Saturdays. This peaceful setting, hidden back from the street in a remote area of Nature, encouraged most to swim in their birthday suits, and to acquire some color sunning on the rocks. The flat surface of the rocks, twenty feet above the water level, presented a clear view to the bottom, at least another twenty feet below the surface. Most would jump, though I liked to do a jackknife, floating down until nearing the surface of the water to open up. A jackknife is easier to control than a straight dive.

A few girls, along with their boyfriends, located themselves on the other side of the quarry.

PRIVATE HOMES with pools existed in Beverly, but only two tempted us, both with ten foot high dives: A North Beverly home belonging to the Hutchison family, the parents of Bill's girlfriend. Two blocks from our grade school was Mr. B's pool, a setting in which we were not welcome. Mr. B's son, Pete, an infrequent member of our group, had informed us, "I'm not allowed to have you guys over." Maybe Mr. B believed we were a bad influence on his son, but the opposite was the case. One night Joe said, "To hell with the old man. Let's go test out his pool." Mr. B's son wasn't with us. More cautious than usual, the five of us who were going to swim, bundled our clothing around our shoes, and placed them next to the pool.

During more than a half hour of five of us swimming, the fifteen others lay around the pool or sat in lawn chairs, laughing, cavorting, and just being noisy. Suddenly the powerful flood lights lit up the entire pool area as though it were daylight. Police appeared from all directions shouting, "Stay where you are. You're all under arrest." The shock from seeing at least a dozen cops left the non-swimmers immobile. They were easy pickings. However the five swimmers had ducked under the surface of the water. While the police were capturing the non-swimmers, the swimmers slid out of the pool without being noticed. I was the first to corral my clothes. As I started to run, I dropped a shoe, and paused to pick it up. My second effort to escape, I dropped the other shoe.

My brother shot by me, heading into a pitch black opening between some tall bushes. Picking up my second shoe, I heard a noise from his direction, like two bodies colliding in a football game (He was the tailback for our high school football team). Frank's welfare was not my problem; mine was to get away. I ran full speed in the same direction, and flew by, catching a glimpse of him entwined on the ground with two cops. In the darkness he had inadvertently run into a police officer with the speed and force of a tailback in a football game, knocking him out cold, only to be jumped by a second cop.

Why were so many police officers called to our swimming party? Yes, we were trespassing, but nothing more. The important Mr. B must have indicated that a gang of ruffians were destroying his property. There were too many cops, though "Thank God" they didn't come with guns drawn.

This was Beverly Hills, the community of important people. The police had to be careful with the local juveniles who could be the sons of those important people: judges, lawyers, big shot politicians, brokers, medical doctors, self-employed store owners, etc.

As an example, after Mass on a Sunday morning, a number of us walked to a small park at 101st and Longwood Drive, where we began to pitch pennies on the sidewalk. When the police arrived, we made no effort to run because we couldn't believe they were going to arrest us over gambling with a few pennies.

The desk sergeant looked down on us as though we were criminals, and began with what we considered inconsequential questions: "I want to know your names and your fathers' occupation. Jack was the first to volunteer his name and his father's work. After Jack gave his name, the sergeant sat back for a minute, and then asked, "What's your father's occupation?"

"My dad's a broker at the Board of Trade."

Then the sergeant asked John, "What's your name and what is your father's occupation?"

John replied, "My dad's a doctor." The sergeant started to become agitated.

"And you over there. What's your father's occupation?"

Pete responded, "He's a lawyer for the Democratic Party."

Finally he asked Bill, "What kind of work does your father do?"

"He's a police captain, and his name's Walsh."

The sergeant paused, looked angrily at the two officers, and stated in a loud voice, "What the hell are you two doing bringing these young men here? Are you trying to cause trouble? Get them the hell out of here."

Returning to the story concerning Mr. B's pool – I had run down the hill away from the pool, reaching Longwood Drive where I ran barefoot in my underpants down the middle of the street, laughing. When finally reaching home I informed Dad, "Frank's in jail."

"How's that? You're here, and Frank's in jail? What happened? How come you're not in jail?"

"We went swimming in Mr. B's pool, and he called the cops on us. Two cops caught Frank, and I got away."

"Did you damage anything?"

"No, we went for a swim in his pool."

"Why did you choose his pool?"

"It was the most convenient."

"Are you telling me the whole story?"

"Yes, there's nothing more to tell."

Dad's statement to the desk sergeant at the police station was, "They were teenagers out for a swim in this heat. They say they haven't damaged anything. Have they?"

At that moment one of the officers walked by and recognized dad.

"Hi Frank. What are you doing here?" Dad explained, and this officer went to the back of the desk-sergeant to whisper something in his ear. I'm sure it had something to do with dad's involvement in the Democratic Party, the dominant party in Chicago for decades.

Then dad said to the sergeant, "The boys inconvenienced Mr. B, and for that they will apologize."

"Thanks, Mr. Cunningham. I'm sure that will suffice," were the final words of the sergeant.

Several years later, sitting outside his Drive Inn on 111th Street called 'Reds (a red head) with some buddies, my brother told the story of our swim in Mr. B's pool. At the end he was asked, "Who were the four swimming in the pool with you?"

"They were Kevin, Jack, Pete, and my brother, Jim. A few of you know them, but for those of you who don't, I'll mention what they've become after serving in WW II: Kevin, a nuclear physicist; Jack, owner of one of the largest car agencies in the country; Pete, an important politician with the Democratic Party, following in the footsteps of his father; and my brother, a psychologist. Our generation had become the next generation of important people."

Most had joined either the Navy or Marines during the war. Some returned home seriously injured; some never returned. However, none were ever the same.

BEVERLY THEATER: We would enter the Theater to see a movie in the pleasant air conditioning. Our strategy was to collect enough money for one person to pay his way in and open one of the emergency doors in the rear to let all the others in. (No alarms or emergency doors existed at that time.) We would climb up a metal ladder to the narrow walkways above the ceiling, enjoy the view of the patrons below, and come down in a more secluded area to avoid being noticed.

6

WINTER RECREATION

In winter, galoshes, somewhat like boots, extending half way to the knee, all rubber, insulated for warmth and snow proof, we adapted to one of our more dangerous activities. One of our group, generally Jack, would fake a fall in front of an oncoming car to force the driver to stop. All of us had cautioned Jack, "You're not giving the driver enough time to put on the breaks; the road's too slippery."

I said to Frank, "What if the driver panics and loses control?"

"Well, that's what it's all about; an adrenaline rush, the more the danger, the greater the rush."

Jack's high-risk action provided the opportunity for several of us to reach the back bumper without the knowledge of the driver; he would pause a few seconds to recover from the frightful ordeal. We'd crouch down, and slide along on our galoshes to begin our game when our host continued. The goal of our game was to knock the feet out from under each other. Often asked, "Didn't the car's exhaust bother you?"

"No, the cold must have reduced the effect of any exhaust."

The game produced much subdued laughter from the rear-end passengers when a victim bit the 'ice'. The 'evil-doer' could be heard, "Got you!" followed by the name (Joe, Pete, Dennis, etc.). The victim would continue hanging on, dragged on his belly until he could get back up on his galoshes, and into the game. Rarely did any victim-player let go; he had to get back into the competition. All the while the driver had no knowledge of the presence of his extra passengers.

However, the one danger from the ice-covered streets was when we would reach a section without ice. Our galoshes wouldn't slide, and we'd be thrown into the air.

Our parents knew nothing of this activity, though I believe Dad would have said, "Be careful!" He never tried to prohibit anything we were into. He knew it would be a waste of time; we would continue doing what we wanted to do anyway. Sliding down the hills of homes situated on Longwood Drive in Beverly on pieces of cardboard, or anything else available became another option, though much less dangerous. From there we graduated to the mild toboggan runs in the park at 87th and Western.

One of the most thrilling, yet safer experiences, took place several miles west on Route 83, professionally managed toboggan runs located in Palos Park (no longer in use). Hundreds stood in long lines since no mechanized hoist existed, limiting the number of rides that could be experienced. Our toboggan could carry six, wrapped together as though one, legs of one over the legs of the one in front, tightly together. As we approached our turn to travel down the run, full of excitement, we faced a trap door controlled by rangers high above the toboggan run, in a structure with picture windows, overlooking the action to ensure the safety of the seating arrangement. The door did not drop! Instead, through

Toboggan Slides, a few miles west of Chicago on Route 83 in Palos Park
(no longer in use)

a loud speaker, a ranger shouted, "Rearrange the legs of the first two; they're not situated safely."

"Frank, from the back position, called out, "Pete, Jack, do what the ranger said."

"Okay!" And the trap door dropped. Down we flew a distance of about a football field, like we did in Riverview on the roller coasters (Silver Streak or the Bobs), reaching a speed of about 60 mph. On the way down Jack and Pete raised their hands in the air, a 'no hands' attitude, while the rest of us shouted and roared. As we slowed down, Frank, in the tail position, threw his weight to the left, causing the toboggan to spin.

Sometimes we would take few of our nephews and nieces to experience the thrill. Carol, a six year old niece, wanted to be in the first position. No fear, full of excitement, she screamed all the way down, and wanted to go a second time in that first slot, but others demanded their turn.

Chicago 1936
Lake Michigan Frozen Solid in Winter

The following week Frank and I thought of a more thrilling activity to heighten the dangers experienced on the toboggan rides. It required Jack's driving talent, a talent that should have been directed to professional race car driving instead of owning a car dealership. In those years when no speed limit existed on Illinois highways outside the city, Jack's addiction to speed became the core of this risky action. Frank and I had built our sleds for use, not for beauty or style. We had selected used 2 x 4s from the wood pile in back of the house, nailed 1 x 6 boards onto 2 x 4 runners with metal strips on the bottom. Our two sleds, tied to the back of Jack's car, could slide along any street without breaking up, even streets without ice.

Some 25 or more of our usual group followed Jack's car to a

paved road on the edge of the city. He pulled our sleds at 35mph, but our fans began to shout, "Faster, Jack, faster."

Someone shouted, "Hey Jack, at a faster speed you could put your car into a full spin."

Jack warmed to this idea, "When I reach 50 mph, I'll put the car into a 360 degree spin."

"Let's go," I shouted, almost shaking with excitement, and fear, but also having a 'devil take care' attitude. The experience was like 'crack the whip' that can be seen on an ice rink, only several times more intense. When Jack spun his vehicle, it didn't stop spinning at 360, but kept spinning like a top. Our sleds rose, flying three feet off the ground, a thrill equal to any roller coaster ride. What awakened us to the deadliness of our ride was when we shot by a fire plug, missing it by a couple of inches.

Afterward Jack said, "God didn't put out the welcome mat yet," and laughed. We offered the use of our sleds to the others, but no one accepted.

On rainy days, no snow or ice, basketball occupied our free time. However the neighborhood outdoor courts weren't playable. Jack's dad, a broker on the Board of Trade, had sired 12 children, and needed his large 3 story home on 99th Street above Longwood Drive. Remembering a church across the street, Jack mentioned, "Across the street from my house is a church with an indoor gymnasium. We could get in through a gym window from the roof, but it would be dangerous because the roof is at least a 45 degree pitch. One of us would need to get to the highest point of the roof, and slide along that point on his butt to where a gym window could be reached."

Frank, my brother responded, "I'll do it." After entering the gym, he opened an emergency door for the rest of us. Since the gym was on the top floor, a considerable distance from the main part of the church for services, we were never noticed.

Another comparably structured church near 114th had a gymnasium on the top floor as well. It also required a dangerous entrance from the roof. This was an alternate gymnasium when religious services in the church on 99th Street were in progress.

7

ATHLETICS WAS OUR LIFE, OUR IDENTITY

My older brother and I occupied our days with sports; the other 'guys' of our group liked to play a sport once in a while, but such didn't dominate their lives as it did for us. Frank and I were opposing captains in our neighborhood sports because we were the two best athletes.

Altercations between us during local softball or football games were common. He would say, "You don't know what you're talking about. End of discussion."

My way in any of our conflicts would be, "I quit." No other option existed because he we a year and a half older, much stronger, a head taller, and at least fifty pounds heavier.

Football became our primary choice; basketball followed; baseball a distant third; and hockey at the tail. The lack of hockey paraphernalia never deterred us from playing. We played sports seasonally: football in the fall, basketball in the winter, baseball in the spring and summer occupied much of our free time.

One spring day recruiting players for a baseball game in our neighborhood, Frank grabbed my catcher's mitt and wouldn't return it. After several minutes of chasing him while he teased, he trotted toward home. I picked up a house brick, and threw it as far as I could. Believing it could never bridge the gap between us, I threw it out of frustration to release some pent-up anger. The flight of the brick appeared as though it would never come down. It did, on Frank's head, knocking him out. I dragged him down the street by his red hair, only to face dad who was sitting on the front steps. I tried to explain what happened in an effort to avoid the consequences, "Dad, I didn't mean to hit him with the brick, but he wouldn't give me my catcher's mitt." Without attending to my explanation, Dad beat the hell out of me.

After football practices and on weekends, many late nights Frank and I competed at punting the football in our back half-acre field. A left footed kicker, he kicked with power, and became the best punter in the state of Illinois. I had to practice more to provide the competition he needed. Being smaller and lighter, I would kick with finesse, always with a spiral to gain distance. Frank made All State honorable-mention for football his senior year. My sophomore and junior years, 1943 and 1944, were not on a par with him. We had a different coach each year, and each coach would take one look at my size, 5'6" and 120 pounds soaking wet, and begin to search for another player to be quarterback. In the basketball season Frank made first team, and I took Gene Kelly's on the first team when he was injured.

Discouraged in football, I decided, when 16, at the end of my junior year, to skip my senior year and matriculate in St. Mary's College, a small college in Winona, Minnesota. I did try out for the football team, and made first team. However, the coach wanted me to play QB, but I wanted to be the tailback (ball carrier), the position I wanted to play in high school. After a week I said to the coach, "I quit!"

A week later he came to me, "You can be the running back if you come back out." I did, though I chose to play without pads, hip and rib pads, because they interfered with my agility and speed.

When the basketball season arrived, I made first team forward, averaging 15 points a game, mostly free-throws from being fouled so much. The height of our tallest player was 6 feet, and if we played the standard style we didn't have a chance. Thus, on my own, I began a one man full-court press, and by two games Bobby, the other small forward, joined me. The coach approved of our input as he recognized the fun and success we were having. Size was no longer that important when we could steal the ball and go in for easy layups. I made Honorable Mention on the All League Team.

Jim Cunningham, flashy Redmen forward, goes up for a spectacular overhead shot in Saturday's game with St. Thomas at St. Paul.

1945-46 St. Thomas ranked #1 nationally with Indiana University.

Within a few months in 1946 the war ended, and I returned to Chicago to earn some money loading freight cars for the Illinois Central RR. During that same year at Christmas time, we were on our way to Evanston by way of the 'L' to watch the pre-league basketball tournament at St. George High School. Recently out of the military Frank had returned home. The trip on the bus from the far SW corner of the city to 63rd and Halsted brought on an argument between us. He ended it temporarily, "We'll settle this when we get off the bus!" I believe he wanted to demonstrate he remained the 'boss.'

We descended from the bus into this second largest shopping center where Bob Hope and Bing Crosby were on stage in a theater. I thought Frank would have calmed down, but not so. He began forcefully pushing me, stating, "I told you what was going to happen!"

"Yes, and I'm not going to take your shit anymore," and threw a hard punch to his face. He never used boxing techniques. With his style of complete aggression, both fists and knees going, he attacked venomously. I had some boxing technique, and avoided Frank's blows by ducking, but he would knee me in the head, or any place he could plant a kick. I threw several punches, always starting with a left jab to keep him from overwhelming me. The battle of two brothers existed without words, without sound, no grunts, no shouts, no pain admitted.

The heavy traffic on both streets was backed up for a couple of blocks, causing a policeman to run toward us to stop the fight. He grabbed both of us by our letter-jackets (the sport jacket with a football on it, or the other jacket with a basketball on it, plus a large letter 'D' for De La Salle High School). We pulled away with such force that he fell down. Forgetting our differences, laughing we ran to the staircase leading up to the Elevated Train Station to continue on our journey to Evanston. We have remained best friends; not even this altercation could change that, remaining avid competitors in most sports.

Several years after WW II, Kevin, a nuclear physicist, recalled this 'fight to end all fights.' In an exaggerated tone of voice for Kevin, accompanied by gesticulations, the guys could feel that the battle of the ages had happened when he stated, "I would never try to stop a fight between those two brothers. That would be risking my own life."

In September1946, seven years of WW II vets entered the University of Illinois. Frank and Bill Lee were two of them entering on the GI Bill. I entered a week later, without the G.I. Bill, needing to find work to pay my way.

Out for football my brother and I could punt the ball as far as Dike Edelmann, the team's official punter and the best punter in the Big Ten. However, this was the time former All-American players were returning from WW II, and unknowns like us were not given much attention.

Following a month of practice I was assigned to the B-team. Misunderstanding what B-team meant, thinking it was something apart from the varsity, I quit. The B-team, I later learned, was composed of those players who would be primary players the following year. Frank had departed earlier to practice his gambling skill, card playing. He played well, often two or three days without a break, and continued this hobby all his life, adding golf when he became aware of the monetary rewards.

Fred Zandier, my roommate and state handball champion, was looking for a partner to compete in doubles. Another member

Fred Zandier, a tail-gunner on a bomber in WWII; survived many missions squeezed into his bubble for hours without being able to relive himself; my roomate and doubles champions in handball at the University of Illinois; a special friend; died 1955

of our fraternity asked Fred if he could be his partner. Fred refused, and asked me instead, "Jim, do you want to be my handball partner?"

"Fred, I've never played the game before! I know nothing about it!"

"Don't sweat it. I'll teach you while we're playing, and we'll win the championship. You can cover the right front quarter of the court, and I'll cover the other three quarters." He was a prophet. We did win the championship while I earned many bumps and bruises from diving after balls hit into my corner.

One Saturday four of us wanted to go for a swim in the university pool, but we found the swim team practicing. I said to the others, "Let's pretend we want to try out for the team." We did, swimming the distances the coach required. I was the only one who qualified for the team, but this team sport didn't interest me. It was football and basketball I wanted to play, but we did enjoy the swim.

My brother and I competed well in horse shoes, a talent we learned during our caddying years; and in fast-pitching softball, our fraternity made the playoffs with my fast-pitching technique, a skill I picked up while playing. In intramural football, my passing and Frank's receiving put our fraternity in the playoffs, but Frank transferred his allegiance from the fraternity to his gambling den (the Ice Rink).

Athletics remained a dominant part of our lives. My brother started his own business on 111th Street, called 'Reds,' limiting the time he could play ball. I became an educator and coach for 50 years.

An experience at the University I remember because I was inquisitive about the sport of gymnastics, similar to my interest in college wrestling, both sports I knew nothing of. Waiting for class outside the physics building next to the gymnastics building, I decided to find out what this sport looked like. I wasn't aware females were involved. I thought it was a male sport. The men were not there, but the girls were. The physical skills were awesome, the flips and twists extremely dangerous. An attractive blonde with a well-sculptured body, caught my eye, not just for her beauty, but because of her talent. The skills of the girls, especially the blonde, left me spellbound. However I made no effort to know any of them personally. "They're out of 'my league,' I said to myself.

Later in the spring, playing catch on the lawn of our fraternity, I happened to notice that blonde walking by. Our fraternity had planned a dance for the following week, for which I had no date. I asked myself, "Could she be a date?" I didn't believe she would 'give me the time of day!' "What do you have to lose?" I asked myself. Taking a deep breath, and throwing caution to the wind, anxiously I walked down to the sidewalk, and politely stated, "Last month when going to my physics class I stopped by your gym to observe your sport. I had never attended a gymnastics meet before. I was impressed! You were magnificent. Our fraternity is having a dance next week, and I would be pleased if you would go with me."

Without hesitating she said, "Yes."

My request was more like jousting with windmills because I could not imagine this attractive young woman accepting! "You don't know my name and I don't know yours, yet you are willing to go with me?"

We exchanged names, and she explained where she lived.

"Three blocks ahead, living at home."

"She's a local girl!" I said to myself.

"Can you give me your address and telephone number so I can call you?" She did!

When she and I walked into the fraternity that night my frat brothers were shocked by her physical beauty and the way she carried herself. Every member wanted to sign her dance booklet. I hurried to put my name in 5 slots, or I would not have had any dances with my own date. Several of the brothers would pass by to ask, "How did you score this beauty for your date?"

"You'll need to visit the gymnastics gym once in a while!"

The entire night was exciting for her as more members tried to put their names on her dance booklet. She was a delight to dance with, so light on her feet. I'm sorry I didn't get a photograph of the two of us. I'm sure that a photo of the 2 of us would have been a keepsake.

Though I wanted to ask her out again, I never had any money, and anyway I would be no competition for the much older affluent students. She was truly a queen for the night.

St. Barnabas School — 1st. grade.

8

CATHOLIC EDUCATION
AND
THE IRISH

O ur parents, graduates of Chicago Catholic High Schools, wanted us to obtain a Catholic education. Though a public grade school existed less than a mile away, we attended St. Barnabas in Beverly Hills, 2.5 miles away.

To be Irish was to be Catholic, and Chicago like Boston, became a bastion of Irish culture and power. Our classmates had names like: O'Connor, Leahy, Flynn, Carroll, Haggerty, Nagel, O'Donnell, Kennedy, Walsh, Cunningham, and O'Connell. Other ethnic neighborhoods (Italian, Polish, Lithuanian, etc.) also had their own parishes with grade schools, while certain Catholic parishes established their own high schools. A large number of Nuns, Priest and Brothers founded and staffed Catholic Schools. There was a time when Catholic School students in Chicago were believed to be as numerous as public school students.

Chicago's city hall became a center of power for the Irish,

most if not all educated through the Catholic School System, with department heads and a large number of politically-appointed employees from the same system.

Most of our classmates at St. Barnabas were 3rd generation Irish, with little knowledge of their forefathers' background, yet they were motivated to seek power. Nearly 100 plus years of being oppressed by the English had influenced their genetic makeup. No different from other ethnicities (Mexicans, Chinese, Puerto Rican, Italians), the Irish had their own neighborhoods, and protected that turf.

The east coast Irish gangs, primarily in Boston and New York, were noted to be as vicious as today's gangs, and even more vicious. However, to my knowledge, Chicago Irish focused more on education than on turf control.

In grade schools all our teachers were nuns and tough disciplinarians, but only a few used physical controls. My older brother's class, more rowdy than usual, had to face Sister Robertine in 8th grade. She was a disciplinarian par excellence, yet preferred boys, especially Frank, even though he was usually the leader of trouble. In his adult life he visited her in Wisconsin at least once a year after her retirement until she died in her 90's.

Robertine became my 8th grade teacher the year following my brother. We had an amiable relationship most of the time because I was one of the 3 top students. However, on one occasion we had a misunderstanding, and I wouldn't agree with how she interpreted it.

In our classroom, on the second floor above the church, the students followed the directive of Robertine to go downstairs. I ascertained later that we were to go into the church, but I thought it was our lunch time, and continued to the lunch room below the church. Recognizing my absence she searched and found me waiting in the lunch room. Assuming I was 'ditching,' she walked me upstairs to our classroom where she directed, "Put your hands down to your side. You deserve a smack."

"Oh no," and put my catcher's mitt up to my face. No way! I'm not letting you hit me!"

"Either you put that mitt down, or go home and bring your father!"

"I'm going home and will return with my father."

In the conference with Dad, Sister Robertine admitted, "After thinking about what Jim said, I concluded his explanation had to be true. He's too honest a student. I had acted too hastily."

In a discussion of the idiosyncrasies of Chicagoans with a protestant couple that had moved to the city from the east coast, I learned of our unique ways of expressing ourselves. For example, "Where do you live?" would be a question, and the answer would be the name of a parish, "In St Sabina parish." A parish indicated a specific area of the city, and the saint's name of such a parish would have been selected from their church in their country of origin in Europe.

Chicago 1939
Winter snow storms would limit all forms of transportation

9

ART OF HITCHHIKING

Hitchhiking was a life style for us, at times exciting, stimulating, but often dangerous. We enjoyed it, even though a few of the dangers were life-threatening. From our grade school years we 'thumbed' rides the 2.5 miles each way, even in the extreme Chicago winter storms when we could be in danger of freezing to death. It would be impossible to see your hand in front of your face. However the thought of missing school was out of the question. To compound the situation, cars if they ever appeared, could not see us.

One unforgettable morning, we walked through a storm to arrive at St. Barnabas grade school, and upon arrival to hear the nun-principal, "School is closed for the day. Gather your belongings and go home." This was one of the worst storms; we weren't sure we could make it home. However, Father Hayes, the assistant pastor, must have been rousted by one of the nuns to search for us. As he drove into the wind-whipped blizzard off Lake Michigan he hunted at the slowest pace possible for fear he would pass without seeing us. When he did find us half frozen, sitting on a curb at Western Avenue, a mile from school, he shouted, "Come on boys. I was beginning to believe I wouldn't find you. I'll take you home!"

To us it was a miracle! We thanked our heavenly Father for keeping the pearly gates closed. He must have been too busy, and we knew He wouldn't want mother to suffer a thousand deaths.

Most of our classmates lived a short distance from school, thus the nuns did not initially recognize the problem the Cunningham boys would face going home, a considerable distance outside the general area.

In those years school buses did not exist; Chicago public transportation had streetcars, but no tracks to our part of the city. A few years later, public transportation, thanks to Dad's influence in the Democratic Party, reached our 'outpost' when public buses were introduced.

From 1942-45 my older brother Frank and I hitchhiked to high school from our far southwest corner of the city to reach the all-boys' Catholic High School taught by the Christian Brothers, located in the midst of a black neighborhood with all its poverty. Our younger brother John joined us two years after me.

Many of our classmates from grade school also hitchhiked to St. Ignatius, taught by Jesuit priests.

I'm not sure how mother maintained her emotional balance while her boys were becoming acquainted with the great city of Chicago. She was a spiritual woman and must have prayed often! How else? She remained at home, not knowing where her free-spirited sons were, what was happening to them, what kind of dangers they were facing.

Today's mothers might find it impossible to accept not knowing the whereabouts of their sons. However, there were no other alternatives for Mother, no car, no cell phones existed. Dad was working in another state. She was alone with her anxieties and worries, and they made her a mother who loved her children more than life itself. We were what she lived for, a fact we did not comprehend until adulthood.

Mother would watch us run next store to Elmer's house to ride with him to the plant where he worked at 55th and Western. She knew nothing of our travels from that point. Frank and I, and later John, enjoyed the excitement of the city. Fifty-Fifth Street was a beautiful boulevard, 2 lanes in each direction, with a parkway in between, as wide as a football field, and extending the entire length of the boulevard, long enough for a few hundred football fields. A large number of fellow students, hitchhiking on the boulevard, would meet their friends, making the morning travel a social event.

Following are examples of six hitchhiking experiences:
1. Motorcycle Cop
2. Blessed by an Old Streetcar
3. John's Jacket
4. Combat Truck Ride
5. The humorous truck driver
6. The Tunnel

MOTORCYCLE COP

On a late afternoon during WWII when football practice ended early, one of the coaches took us to 39th and Ashland on Chicago's south side, where we began to 'thumb' south on Ashland. Always standing a few feet into the road to be clearly noticed, we waited patiently for about ten minutes. Suddenly a motorcycle cop pulled up, from where we didn't know. He kicked down his stand, and motioned, "Come here!"

We obeyed his command, "No hitchhiking on my streets!"

"Yes officer," we politely responded, and moved out of the street to the sidewalk, as the cop motored on south, in the direction we were headed.

I said to Frank, "Who in the hell does he think he is? In all the years we've been thumbing rides, we've never been bothered by Chicago cops."

Frank answered, "He's going south, so we'll go west, but only after he's out of sight". Within five minutes, Frank noticed, "Here comes a truck! Do you think you can catch it on the run?"

"Sure, let's go!" Running at full speed I caught up to the truck, and pitched myself up onto the tail gate. Frank followed easily. Our truck carried us one mile west to Western Avenue, a busy street that paralleled Ashland.

The street was one of our preferred with plenty of traffic. Within a couple of minutes we had a ride to 55th Street, the location of Gage Park, where we played in a softball league in the summer.

Immediately we went to work hustling a ride further south when we spotted that same motorcycle cop heading west on 55th Street in our direction. He didn't notice us at first, but when he did he pointed his 'cycle' directly at us. Without a word, the two of us ran into the park, as though we could read each other's mind, and calculated the best way to avoid this aggressive egotistical cop.

"You two won't get away," he shouted while he rode his cycle into the park. However, zigzagging on the run through the bushes, Frank ran in one direction and I in another, laughing loudly, irritating him all the more. It was a game of 'catch me if you can!' Finally he gave up chasing us, and went on his way south, the same direction we were going.

I said to Frank, "I think he's given up. What do you think?"

"Yeah, he can't spend his whole day chasing us."

Rides were coming quickly, but not much distance. We returned to Western Avenue and caught a ride to 63rd Street, only a mile distance. Frank, in the middle of the front seat and me on the door, I opened it to get out, to be confronted by the same cop kicking down the stand of his cycle, stating with a grin that filled his entire face, "Now I got you!"

Immediately I shut the door and locked it, while at that exact fraction of a second Frank was rising out of his place, jumping over the front seat to the back seat, and opening the back door behind the driver, with me on his tail.

These quick moves would be more amazing if the reader knew each of us carried a leather case filled with school books.

In those days backpacks didn't exist. We reached the other side of the street laughing so hard we almost fell down, and continued walking the four blocks to 67th Street to be sure the cop had given up. Frank said, "Let's head west to Kedzie Avenue."

"Sure." It was another street paralleling Ashland and Western. At home I commented about our ride, "I can't imagine that poor driver picking up any more hitchhikers. I'm sure he was shocked, and probably afraid." Years later we still laugh each time we recall that spiffy cop standing there, when the door was slammed in his face.

THE BLESSING OF AN OLD STREETCAR

It was a dark night, around eight o'clock in the fall of 1944, after a long football practice. P.J., Frank, and I were trying to get a ride from our usual corner, outside our high school at 35th and Michigan. We relied on our football letter-jackets to communicate who we were, but the street light was out, making us almost invisible.

After some 30 minutes without a ride, my older brother Frank said, "Let's take any ride, even a short one. We could be here all night." We had 14 miles through most of the Chicago's south side to get home.

"I don't know Frank. That's risky, but I do know that mother will begin to worry." We finally accepted a ride to 51st Street, a corner not known to us, four blocks short of our usual safe zone.

Reaching the 51st Street corner, I said to Frank, "I'm anxious here. Maybe we should walk the four blocks to 55th Street."

"Let's give it a try first. P.J. and I can go back in the shadows while you thumb a ride. We've a better chance with only one of us out here."

"Okay." Aware my size would not be threatening, Frank and P.J. went back in the dark between two buildings. P.J. was one of our tackles, a lumbering giant at least six feet five inches and weighing 280 pounds. Any driver would think twice about giving us a ride. Thus, P.J. and Frank could not be seen.

Within a brief period, a thin black, taller than P.J., approached, stood in front of me, and in a slow drawl stated, "Hey man, what you doin in my neighborhood?" I could feel danger from my head to my toes.

Stuttering from nervousness, I responded, I'm trying to get a ride home. I don't have any more money." The back of his right hand crashed across my face, nearly driving me back into the traffic.

"You'd better move on. This ain't no place for a white boy!"

"Why don't you tell that to my buddies back there?"

Suddenly a switchblade appeared in his hand, a quick silent move as he popped it open. He started in their direction, but reconsidered when he noted P.J.'s size along side of my muscular brother. He changed direction to enter a pool hall we hadn't noticed before, a hangout for young blacks.

Recognizing the danger, Frank said, "Let's get out of here. We can catch a streetcar on State Street." State Street was two blocks away, two long blocks away considering the gang after us. As we expected, some 20 youths were soon in pursuit. Frank shouted, "P.J., keep going!" To give P.J. more time, Frank and I picked up rocks from the alley between Wabash and State Street to throw at our pursuers, delaying them briefly. P.J. flagged down the streetcar on State Street, and as the streetcar began to move forward with P.J. on board, Frank and I tore after it. I grabbed the handle on one side of the stairs while Frank grabbed the handle on the other side.

The three of us faked a prolonged search for money. I was first. "I think I have enough change for the three of us." After a couple of minutes without a word, I shrugged my shoulders, and showed my empty palms. "Nothing!" I said.

Frank asked P.J., "Do you have any money?"

"Nope, I used my extra money to buy an extra dessert for lunch."

Frank turned his pockets inside out. "I don't have any money either."

The streetcar stopped at 55th Street where we jumped off. The heavy built Irish conductor, aware of what we were doing, chose to become a willing participant. In a jovial voice, he shouted out to us when we had distanced ourselves, "Anything to help some fine Irish lads from the Catholic school to escape from that gang back there," and waved goodbye. He had recognized us by our football letter-jackets."

Approaching home, and calmed down after our big escape, Frank said, "An adrenaline surge is a better high than any chemical one."

Streetcars lined up on State Street in front of Marshall Field

JOHN'S JACKET

It was a school night that Frank, John, and I were making our way home from the football practice field behind White Sox Park , the closest corner with a red light. This corner didn't provide a ride for twenty minutes, so we decided on our streetcar ploy. Without any money between the three of us, we entered at the front of the streetcar along with the other passengers. Frank, the oldest, always watched out for me, and I watched out for John, my younger brother. John had a vision problem from birth, and moved more cautiously than his two brothers. Our goal was to ride the streetcar to the 55th Street Boulevard where we could easily hitch a ride west.

The entrance to the streetcar was in the front, across from the motorman. The exit was in the rear where the conductor collected fares. On the Wentworth streetcars passengers paid when leaving. Unwisely we stationed ourselves too close to the front door rather than somewhere in the middle. The motorman must have guessed what we were planning.

Arriving at 55th Street we moved forward. John was to shoot out the entrance door first, then me, and lastly Frank. With his vision problem, John was too slow enabling the motorman to grab John's jacket off his arm, while I was pushing him forward out the door. Frank stayed on the streetcar to recover John's jacket from the motorman, but waited until the streetcar was at full speed. Grabbing the jacket, he was assaulted by the motorman who jumped up out of his seat and attacked Frank to take back the jacket. "Give me that jacket," he shouted, while the streetcar continued lumbering down the street.

The motorman was no match for my brother, an all-state football player, yet away from his console he continued the battle up on his feet for two blocks. Imagine the fear of the passengers watching the motorman wrestle with a passenger, while the streetcar ran on its own! Siding with my brother they knew nothing of the motorman's theft of John's jacket.

The passengers began to panic, shouting at him to get back in his seat.

Two men took charge, each taking an arm of the motorman, forcing him back in his seat. Frank retreated to the middle of the car with the jacket. At 63rd Street the motorman stopped the streetcar in front of the police station without opening the doors, while he shouted to a policeman coming out of the station, "Help, I need help with a guy in here."

John and I continued hitchhiking rides home, while Frank was arrested. When we arrived home to inform Dad of Frank's arrest, Dad indicated, "I've just finished talking to the police station at 63rd and Wentworth. They tell me your brother has been arrested. I'm about to drive there to claim him." Not waiting to hear our story, he wanted to get to that police station in a hurry, believing Frank had gotten into serious trouble. At the Police Station Dad was informed that Frankie had not paid his fare on the streetcar.

"And for that he has been arrested, not paying his fare? How much was that?"

"A nickel," the sergeant answered.

"You mean he's being arrested for a nickel?" Dad responded in a humorous tone of voice.

The sergeant, embarrassed from this trivial offense, apologized, "Sorry Mr. Cunningham! That motorman made a big deal out of it. I hope you'll accept my apology!" On the drive home Frankie, still with John's jacket, related the complete story, while dad had a good laugh. Our father could recognize how trivial this event was. There were times he shared his own teenage escapades with us, and they weren't that much different.

COMBAT TRUCK RIDE

I was still alive through the multitude of dangerous altercations with truck drivers, but this experience was one of the most death-defying of all. When relating this story, Frank reminded me, "I wasn't with you on that one. You were on your own."

I was aboard this truck when suddenly another teenager jumped up on the truck with me. I didn't know him, nor had I ever seen him before, but I welcomed his company, sharing my first name with him, and he in turn, sharing his. "My name is Richard, though I prefer Rich."

Within a couple of minutes it became obvious that Rich wasn't accustomed to riding on the back of trucks. It's an art, and since I had become somewhat of a pro, I offered, "Do you want some advice as to how to survive back here?"

"Yeah, this truck is real bumpy, yet you seem to ride easily."

"It's the knees that make it easy." Always keep the knees bent a little to absorb the bounces, like a spring. Never straighten your legs; keep those knees bent, like this."

"Like this?!

"Yeah, you've got it." And, with a little more practice he had it.

The truck driver, through his rear view mirror, spotted us on the back, and began zigzagging, rocking the truck side to side in an effort to shake us off. However, my new companion weathered the storm easily with the one lesson I gave him. In fact we laughed and talked as the driver became more and more extreme in his efforts to shake us off. Finally, in desperation, he made a sharp turn to the left on two wheels into a side street. The truck rode precariously on those two wheels for about 20 yards, while the driver tried to slow down to recover control. Experiencing a degree of anxiety, I said to Rich, "Let's get off before both of us are hurt." I went first, with Rich close behind. Both of us slid on the pavement, leaving a few scrapes. This driver had become too extreme, and within the blink-of-an-eye, the truck tipped over.

We hurried up to the truck to check on the driver, when we noticed him trying to slide out his window. He did exit safely, obviously upset and angry, and thus, we stopped short to assess whether it was wise to risk helping him. Almost out of the truck he shouted, "You little bastards, I'm going to kick the shit out of both of you!"

I knew better than to stay around, and warned Rich, "we better get the hell out of here in a hurry."

A good distance away, shaking his head, Rich said, "That's my last ride on the back of a truck."

71ST STREET

Saturday morning on our way to football practice, our first ride carried us to a light at 71st and State, where we stationed ourselves on the safety island (a sidewalk in the middle of the street with a three foot high cement mound in front to protect those waiting for a streetcar). Few vehicles on a non-working day, only trucks, we were in a hurry, aware of the penalties for being late to practice. Our coaches had learned their heavy-handed tactics well from their college playing years.

A large truck, stopping for the light, completely empty, such that the driver had a full view of whatever might happen in the back, but we decided to ride his truck whether or not he liked it. When the light turned green and the truck began to move forward slowly. I jumped up on the tailgate, seating myself backward. Frank, waiting for me, followed. In his motion of hopping up on the truck, the driver hit the brakes. My brother disappeared under the truck when jammed against the tailgate. I jumped off to check on him. "Are you okay, Frank?" I had also glanced in the direction of the truck driver when I jumped off his truck, and noticed him having a good laugh."

That 'son of a bitch' had purposely braked to catch Frank in the motion of jumping up. Again the driver started up slowly, still laughing. His laughter lasted only a few seconds because, as Frank told me later, "You ran up to the truck, opened the cab door, flew in and punched him, alternating fists, left, right, several times in the face."

I was beyond fear, in a state of rage, adrenaline taking over and demanding action. I was not aware of running to the truck, or punching the driver. Frank added, "The driver didn't have time to protect himself, nor stop the truck. It kept going forward slowly on its own until it hit a curb a short distance down the street, with the driver sitting there, not moving."

When Frank explained to me what I had done, I said, "I'm going to finish what I started."

Holding his broken hand, he replied, "No, he's had enough."

And, we continued hitching rides or flipping trucks to be on time for practice. When we arrived, Frank knowing he would not be given any slack because of his hand, had it tapped by the athletic trainer, and kept it taped for several days until the pain subsided.

No one could hurt a brother without facing the consequences.

STREETCAR AT 63RD

The old Chicago streetcars ran on fixed rails like most streetcars, and could not deviate from those rails. However, at 63rd and State, a streetcar heading south had to follow rails that curved about 15 feet to the right in order to pass through a tunnel under train tracks. Any vehicle coming out of that same tunnel heading north, had to curve in the opposite direction. The driver of a vehicle had a degree of flexibility while the motorman of the streetcar did not.

In our travels to and from high school, we had begun to incorporate oil trucks as one of our forms of transportation because the back ladder made it easy to stand and not be noticed by the driver.

I remember so vividly a specific oil truck ride we took south on State Street, and continued beyond 55th Street because the truck beat the light. 55th Street Boulevard was our usual 'safe route heading West. When reaching 63rd Street we encountered a tunnel under some rail road lines. I said, "Frank, this curve is dangerous!"

"Yeah, but there hasn't been any accidents here that I've ever heard of," Frank answered, making light of my concern. Traveling south on State Street had never been one of our 'safe routes.' The street had too many large holes, and the traffic was primarily trucks.

Some time later, we heard about the accident at that

intersection. Reading about the story in the paper, I commented to mother, "I've always been concerned about that curve." However, I didn't let her know how and why I was concerned. How could she not worry when her boys were away challenging life to the fullest? She would have forbidden us to hitchhike. However, even if she did forbid us, we would have continued.

The accident was horrendous! An oil truck, heading north exited from the tunnel under the train tracks, facing a streetcar heading south before it made the right turn. The oil truck ran head on into a streetcar. The truck split wide open, raw oil flying into and over the streetcar, sparks causing a fire that turned into a holocaust, frying almost everyone in it. Nearly 100 people became ashes.

No wonder oil truck drivers are paid twice the rate of truck drivers. The danger is so much greater. However, the accident did not deter us from flipping up on oil trucks when necessary. Nevertheless we never again traveled in the direction of that tunnel under the train tracks at 63rd and State.

10

WORK

During the Great Depression finding a job was almost impossible, until WW II when work was available for any warm body of any age. Twelve to fifteen million men and women were in the military, and a majority of the remaining able-bodied women were employed in munition plants.

Families had adjusted to the difficult times. Our father, not only encouraged my two brothers, Frank and John, and me, to find work, he required it. His philosophy required that all family members participate in the needs of the family.

In 1934 we began selling magazines, and in1937 Frank and I, ten and nine years old respectively, transitioned to caddying in Ridge Country Club, within the city limits of Chicago, at 106th and California. We found a short cut at 107th street through the western fence of the golf course.

As B-class caddies we earned $0.90 a round; and when we reached A-class the following year we earned $1.10 a round. A number of caddies came from Beverly and Morgan Park, though most were from Mount Greenwood or other more distant areas.

During the long hours waiting at the caddie shack, most of us occupied ourselves in games of horseshoes, softball, and a few insignificant activities. A group of eight from the 111th Street area of Mount Greenwood, rarely participating in sports, preferred to amuse themselves by annoying others, especially the smaller caddies. On an afternoon when my older brother was out on the course caddying, one of the gang named Tom ran into me.

Hey, what's up Tom?"

"I didn't see you," he grumbled.

But within a few minutes Tom ran into me again, more physical than the first time, establishing a clear indication I was to be their prey that day. "Are you looking for trouble, Tom?" I asked. I could feel my heart pounding, blood pressure mounting, and my entire body readying for violence.

"With a little guy like you, why not?" he laughed. This was to be my entrée into the male world of violence and conflict. Only nine years old I could be dangerous if my anger rose to rage.

Making every effort to appear calm I offered, "We can go outside the fence and settle this!" Tom readily agreed.

This would be my first official fight, and it had to be off the golf course property. A fight on the property warranted a suspension. A number of fight fans walked the two blocks through the golf course to arrive outside the fence between the 15th and 16th holes.

While walking, without recognizing what I was doing, I was punching the palm of my left hand with my right fist to control stress. A few fans made an effort to distract me, but I waved them away in an irritated voice, "Let me alone; I need to think?" It was all I could do to control myself.

Later I answered the question, "Why wouldn't you talk?"

"I was planning my fight strategy."

Fights of this kind would begin slowly, causing one of the older fans, eager to see blood, to take charge and coerce one of the combatants to accept a small piece of wood (anything) placed on his shoulder. Knocking the item off the shoulder by the other fighter led to a retaliatory push, and back-and-forth pushing would escalate to punches.

In this situation an older fan asked, "Which one of you will have this stick placed on his shoulder?" Generally neither wanted it.

However, in a halting voice that conveyed anxiety, maybe fear as well, I answered, "You can place it on my shoulder." My strategy began when my adversary knocked the stick off. Instead of following protocol and pushing him in return, I exploded in violence, hitting him with full force, right, left, right, left, and the fight was over in ten seconds. The gang of eight never bothered me again.

After five years caddying in the warm outdoor summers, and 13 years old, I had become the number one A-class caddie, but no longer legally eligible to work. There were other 13 year olds facing this same legality. The State of Illinois passed a law requiring the minimum age to be fourteen. The concept of a 'grandfather clause' had not been invented.

A couple of us tried farm labor on a 'truck farm' west of Chicago. Surviving for that one day, we came to the conclusion this was no work for us; it was slave labor.

Within a week, through Dad's involvement with the Democratic Party, he found work for me in a public cemetery on 111th Street, referred to as 'Evergreen Cemetery Built like a Park.' Driving there with Dad to meet the maintenance supervisor, my elbow out the window, I appeared taller. Dad settled the employment arrangement, ending a brief discussion with Herman, the supervisor, "Jim can come tomorrow, if that's okay with you?"

"Yup, that'd be gud," he responded in his Swedish accent. The next day I bicycled to the cemetery, and when dismounting, my small size stopped the supervisor as he stared at this little kid who looked no more than ten, and not five feet tall. After a pause he shook his head and commented, "I thought you were bigger!"

Yet he put me to cutting the grass around the graves with an electric trimmer. After a month, when I became skilled and less careful, I opened myself to injury, swinging the trimmer back and forth, cutting closer and closer to my feet without moving them. Suddenly the trimmer gashed one of my shoes. However, with steel-toes limiting penetration, my foot was safe.

The next summer, Frank and I, along with eight others of our group, applied at the Wisconsin Steel Mills. Though being the smallest and the youngest, I was assigned to the most dangerous job, removing bricks from the deep hole that served as an oven for heating the large ingots. I can still be emotional when describing this work. "Men (another teenager and me) were sent down a ladder into this hell-hole lined with bricks that served to heat nine ingots red hot, each three feet square and nine feet long. After multiple uses the bricks would become brittle, and had to be removed while still hot, so hot a man could not remain in that hole for more than a minute or two due to a lack of oxygen, and his shoes would smolder. Breaking down the worn bricks and removing them was the job for two of us, taking turns. Frank and the other guys were placed at a variety of sites. I did ask myself, "Why did the boss give me the most dangerous job?"

After two weeks I said to my partner, "I've had enough," and went to the boss to complain, "I've been at this job for two weeks. Don't you think it's time for others to do this dangerous work? I want to have my health when returning to school this fall."

He replied, "It sounds like you need a week's vacation. Come back after that." Reluctantly I took the vacation and returned, but never again had to climb down into that hole.

The older experienced steel workers, with years in the mill, would be difficult to assign to this work because: first, they were essential at other important sites; and secondly, as members of the union they would seek the support of the union to resist the transfer. Young inexperienced workers, like me, could be placed in low-skilled work, often the most dangerous. We were only temporary and non-union. When a temporary employee had a gripe, the manager could sit back in his chair, and say, "Gee, that's tough!"

In my sophomore year, and Frank's junior year in De La Salle High School at 35th and Wabash on Chicago's south side, after football and basketball seasons ended by early March, we found part-time work after school, sweeping and cleaning up messes in the Goldenrod Ice Cream plant at 39th and Michigan, a half mile from school. It was easy work, but we couldn't stay away from the free ice cream, each eating at least a gallon every day. After two weeks we chose to end our ice cream feasts before we became blimps, and moved a couple of blocks west on 39th Street to the Link Belt aluminum plant, doing maintenance. This part time job carried us until the end of the school year.

That summer, six of our group applied for work loading freight cars on the Illinois Central Railroad, situated east of downtown Chicago, in the railroad yard under the Outer Drive, a

De La Salle High School at 35ᵗʰ and Wabash, Chicago, built in 1889, taught by Christian Brothers

highway running parallel to Lake Michigan. We didn't hesitate to switch employment to any job that paid more. This employment also provided an important benefit, a free pass on their passenger trains.

Within two days loading boxcars, one of the older stevedores took me under his wing to give me some tips, "Stevedore-work is better than trucking because when boxes of candy or other eatables come to your boxcar you can drop one on something sharp to put a hole in it, and we can all eat." After a pause, he continued, "And, when merchandise isn't coming to your boxcar, you can build a wall to go behind and sleep." Because of my small size, older workers became my mentors, and protected me from potential injuries.

However, I started as a trucker (the one who brings items to a boxcar for the stevedore to store), and again an older trucker mentored me, "Stay away from those huge circular crates of cheese (four feet in diameter and three feet high) if at all possible; they're heavy. The weight can reach 1,000 pounds, but when you can't avoid your turn, keep your handles low, or that cheese crate will flip you over the top." At fourteen, two years underage, and 110 pounds at most, my size and weight were barely enough to balance the poundage. I did learn to keep the handles as close to horizontal as possible, often scrapping the legs along the floor. As confidence rose I took for granted I could haul any cheese crate; but one of the crates did flip me several feet in the air. Athletically, I managed to complete a full flip, and land on my feet.

Shaking all over I shouted, more to myself, "This crate must weigh more than 1,000 pounds!"

My experienced friend approached to warn me again, "Check the poundage listed on the side of the crate, and don't take more than the 1000 pounds. See here, yours weighs 1,150 pounds. Your body size and weight won't give you enough leverage to balance more than the 1,000 pounds."

It was a pleasant summer when for three months our group earned good money, enough to buy our own hot lunches in the caboose-diner next to the freight docks, and turn over the remainder at home.

That fall we continued to play on the football team. Frank, the primary ball carrier for the second successive year, built with large muscular legs, had the strength to power his way through the opposition's line. I was one of the second stringers who were blessed to serve as fodder for the starting team. I did suffer at least two concussions that year. In those days such injuries weren't given much attention. The coach's attitude, "Get up and shake it off."

The basketball season followed football, and our Saturdays were free, but we needed to work. One of our uncles, employed with Railway Express, informed dad we could work loading trucks for his outfit. However, we had to get up at 4a.m. to travel on public transportation, and arrive by 6 a.m. at the loading dock to put our names on the 'Bums List,' then sleep on a picnic table until the boss appeared. A Bum's List was so called because the majority of men wanting to work were alcoholics from skid row (every other physically able man in the military), and would be paid at the end of that day with cash money in a small yellow envelop.

Mixing with these men was an education. We heard many stories about their successful lives before ending on skid row. Some wanted to hide from families or to run from pressures. The reasons were many. Sad to say, a day's wages could carry an alcoholic living on skid row for a few days on cheap wine while eating free in a charity kitchen; and when out of cash he would migrate back to the docks in the hope of being rehired. Not all that presented themselves would be hired; a limited number were needed, and no more names were called.

It was important to get there as early as possible to be among the first arrivals to sign the list. I always wore a turtle-neck sweater to appear more muscular. When the boss arrived and picked up the list, he would stand on top of one of the picnic tables to select men for work. First he would look around to select other than skid row bums. Frank and I, bright eyed and healthy looking, would be selected early; then the boss would refer to the list, calling one name at a time.

"You two Cunninghams ready to work? (Always there each Saturday morning, he knew our names.) Our uncle Bob had put in a good word for us.

"Yes."

"Here's your work-pass," he shouted, and we were employed that day.

Back in the neighborhood we advised some of the other guys where they could earn quick money, and be paid at the end of the day. They were interested until we explained, "You'd be on a hiring list with skid row bums."

"No thanks." They all said. They didn't want to mix with the men coming from skid row, and they didn't like getting up so early in the morning. We didn't have a choice; Dad would wake us.

On one of our Saturdays, Frank hid two animal-skin vests under his coat, and when back home a short time, a Railroad Express private detective appeared at our front door. Politely he said, "I'd like to recover those vests."

He accepted the vests, said, "Thanks," and departed. Nothing more happened, and we continued on the Bum's List. We wondered how that detective knew Frank had taken those vests.

The summer between Frank's junior year and his senior year we returned to the Illinois Central Railroad. However, nothing significant occurred; Frank's thoughts centered on being able to finish his senior year. Missing two credits to graduate, he found one credit by enrolling in a newly established typing class, offered at 7:15 a.m. Brother Morris started this early-bird class out of concern for a number of seniors who lacked a credit to graduate, and they would be inducted into the military without a high school diploma. Lacking 2 credits Frank also matriculated in a night class in Englewood High School. It was 1945, and the draft was calling!

He was assigned to the Great Lakes Naval Station the day

after his graduation, and became one of the last of our group to enter the military. I thought to falsify my age and join up too, but Dad wouldn't hear of it. "You're too young, and your mother and I are not ready to sacrifice another son." I had always associated with older guys, and now all had been drafted.

As an option I had thought of bypassing my senior year and going to college. Many small colleges were having financial problems due to a lack of enrollment. St Mary's College in Winona, Minnesota thought of a solution: offer the top 10% of the junior class of any Catholic High School to earn college credits that first year, while duplicating those same credits for the senior year as well. However I let that bargain pass when I found a high paying job on the National Gas Pipe Line, located in the northeastern section of Chicago, near the steel mills.

Again I had the most dangerous job in this business. I would crawl into the tunnels under roads through which the gas line had been inserted. George, my working partner, and I, flipped a coin to determine which part of the job each would perform, and I lost. George was to shovel sand into a machine that looked like a cement mixer, and that machine would force-feed the sand through a fire hose. I would drag the hose into the tunnel, sliding on my belly, and lie on top of the gas pipe to direct the flow of sand into the air space around the natural gas pipe. I could hear and feel the cars and trucks rumbling overhead, living with the fear that they could cause a cave-in. Each day for a month I crawled into one of those tunnels with the anxiety this could be the day I would be buried alive. For hours in the darkness, lying on top of the hose directing the sand, I often fell asleep. Once, only once, did I fall deeply asleep, to be awakened by the sand as it packed against my face. Waking up petrified, I thought, "This is the end."

After George and I had filled up all the gas line tunnels, ending the need for this dangerous work, rather than be thankful, the boss called us into his office. Without mincing words, he said, "I don't need you two any longer." He could have placed us on another part of the job, but he didn't seem to like two teenagers around (except to do the dirty work).

Thus the college option came to mind again, and became much more attractive. Dad came to an agreement with St. Mary's college administration about how the cost of room, board, and tuition would be paid. I would work two jobs at the college: one to manage the switch board, and a second, to ring the bell for class attendance. I was also assigned to a dormitory room for four students. This 4 student dorm room reduced the expense some more, and Dad paid the remainder. I began classes at the end of May, 1945. If the war continued, attending college would be an exemption.

As a 16 year old entering college, I did not earn the grades I had earned in high school. I wasn't as serious about class work as I should have been; at times setting up bowling, using pop bottles for pins and a baseball as a bowling ball. I took up ping pong seriously, but could never beat Dave Lee, from south side China Town at 22nd Street. Dave and his brother had won the state doubles championship. Nevertheless I won most of our billiard competitions.

In August I joined the football team, quit after a week due to a disagreement with the coach, but returned a few days later at the request of the coach. He conceded, "You can be the running back."

Nevertheless, the equipment room had few shoes, none fitting me. Other equipment for a person my height and weighing also were too large. To provide a concrete example of my size, on our game trips in the old school bus, I slept comfortably up in the open luggage area.

I did accept a larger pair of shoes, but refused rib and hip pads because they would slow me down. Speed was essential to avoid being injured. The over-large shoes contributed to a broken ankle during the second half of the first game, but I continued playing to the end. Walking a week on the swollen and painful ankle forced me to confer with the school doctor who diagnosed multiple breaks. Like six others with castes from broken legs that year the doctor put on a caste, scribbling a terminal date on the caste.

It was always important to me to demonstrate I could endure pain without complaining, and to be among the best athletes as well. Only in this way could I be accepted by the older guys.

However basketball trials were coming up, and I wanted to play. Thus changing the terminal date from 4 weeks to 2 weeks made that possible to make the team (with a mild limp). Without height we lost every league game. To better the odds, I started a one-man full court press. Most opposing teams had starting lineups that averaged 6'5". When Bobby Skemp, the other forward my size, joined my full-court-press, the opposition's tall players found difficulty keeping the ball away from two midgets zipping around them, and frequently using behind-the-back passes. Where we learned this passing technique I don't know. I do know it was very effective in avoiding interceptions. We did come close to defeating St. Thomas in our gym, a team ranked number one in the country with Indiana University. Noting the success of our full-court-press, our team spirit at a high, and the excitement of the fans, our coach approved of our aggressiveness.

A transfer from Notre Dame, Bambanek, at 6'5", could play

non-league games. With his height and our full court press, we won every non-league game, and at the end of the season I was selected to the All-Conference team.

In February 1946, after finishing the academic year in college, I was given credits for the full year in both college and high school.

I returned to Chicago, where I went back to work at the Wisconsin Steel Mills with my younger brother John. For some unknown reason one of the older youths, born and raised in the steel mill area, began picking on John. Because of John's vision problem, if in a fight, he would be beaten badly; I could never accept someone picking on a brother. Walking up to this bully, a half a head taller and some 3 years older, I warned him, "Don't mess with my brother!"

"You little 'shit,' you want to take me on? We can go under the rollers and settle this." He was aware that a fight could cause him to lose his job, a life-time job for him; no one would notice a fight under the rollers, one of the most dangerous locations in the steel mills. Rollers compressed red hot steel ingots to varying sizes, while hot pieces would drop off and fall into the trench under the rollers.

"No, let's settle it here!" My job was only temporary, and if I lost it, I could easily find another. My strategy was always confrontational, forcing an adversary to think what he might be getting into. I always removed my partial of four front teeth, to present a ghoulish appearance like someone who could be vicious enough to feed on the dead.

"Forget it!" my adversary said, and walked away.

After 2 months at the steel mills, John went back to school, and I went to work again for the Illinois Central Railroad. It would be my first experience with a union representative who appeared at my boxcar. "Hey young fella, any man working for the railroad always joins the union, and you've been here long enough to be considered a full-timer."

After a few minutes of talking, David, a coworker approached, "What's up Jim?"

"This guy wants me to join the union."

"Oh, maybe I could join too!" David said.

The union man stated firmly, "We don't accept Negroes!"

That aroused my anger, "Well, I don't join any union that won't accept my black friends." The union talk was over.

This black, an x-sailor recently back from WW II, along with a black army buddy named Rudy, always dressed in their military garb, and were two real friends to me.

As a stevedore I would receive freight trucked into my boxcar. A confrontation with a third black, Jesse, demonstrated their friendship. Trucking a Studebaker motor to my boxcar, Jesse, either carelessly or on purpose, dropped it on my feet, and I shouted at him, "You 'asshole,' you want to crush my feet?" He didn't hurt me because of my steel-toed shoes, but he could have.

"Who you think you be, calling me that f.... name?" He took a step toward me, and out came a switch blade.

David and Rudy, catching sight of what was happening, came running, and confronted my attacker, "What you doing, brother?" They took the knife from him, and beat him up; he never returned.

His departing words were, "You two protecting this f..... white honky against a brother?"

I wasn't able to comprehend the racial attitude of the union rep. Dad had taught us that unions protected workers from unfair treatment. Then two blacks befriended me and protected me from a third black. Yet, I never had a black friend before, nor did I expect a black to protect me. My values were being challenged. What had we learned from this war to end all wars?" I asked myself. "A war we battled as brothers to find peace, but did we learn?" The blacks I began to know did learn, but the country hadn't. This was the real world I was encountering, and it wasn't so nice. It remained racist!

CHAPTER

11

A DELICIOUS WATERMELON

On a hot summer night in Chicago, three of us, all teenagers, with nothing to do, arrived at the corner of Vincennes and 95th Street, where watermelons were on sale in a closed-up gas station. "Now what can be done with a watermelon besides eat it?" I asked, more to myself.

Cost had never been a problem because we never paid for anything, and since I was a little more adventurous than the others, I said, "I'm off," and grabbed one of the melons, put it under arm like a football, and acted like a ball carrier as I ran in the direction of the street. Looking behind me to check if anyone had noticed, I ran into the side of a squad car stopped on the corner for a red light. My upper body passed into the open window on the off-driver's side, as though I wanted to sit on that officer's lap.

Quite shocked he pushed me back out shouting, "What the hell are you doing?"

"I was trying to catch that streetcar over there," I answered in a soft apologetic voice, pointing at it on the other side of the squad car. This spontaneous response originated from the many CYA (cover your ass) experiences of the past.

"Sorry," I said, and ran around the back of the squad car. Grabbing the hand bar at the back stairs while the streetcar started up, I noticed the police no longer watched me. They had believed my story, it was so far-fetched. Who could extemporaneously make up such a 'whopper?'

My two friends looked on in amazement as this scene evolved.

As only mischievous teens could comprehend, they knew I wouldn't stay on that streetcar any more than I needed to give the appropriate image to the police. When I recovered my breath I said to the conductor, "I don't have any money, not even a couple of coins." So, the conductor casually pulled the cord to stop the car at the next block. My two partners followed as fast as they could run.

We began to tear at the melon with our hands after dropping it on the pavement to crack it open. While eating a few of the parts Dave said, "Don't throw away the rind. We can blast some cars with it." Tim threw a small piece at a passing car. Dave threw another small piece at the following car. As that piece splattered against the car, we found what we were looking for. Our fun intensified as we enjoyed scaring drivers. Like so many teenagers we had not "walked in the moccasins" of our victims, and had not recognized the danger that could occur if the driver lost control. Wisdom we lacked, and the fear of being arrested never entered our minds.

Considering more intense levels of excitement we climbed onto the roof of Walgreen's Drug Store on 95th Street. The roofs of the four other stores were as one with Walgreens, each roof separated by a three foot wall. From up there we continued throwing watermelon rinds at passing cars with accuracy. A couple of drivers, surprised and probably shocked, braked to a screeching halt. Little did we know however that Walgreens had been robbed through the skylight the previous week. Someone notified the police that another 'robbery' was in progress, so the police appeared, surrounded the stores and beamed floodlights over the roof tops. Guns were at a ready- position when the police captain shouted a warning through a bullhorn, "Come down with your hands up. This is the police captain speaking."

Tim whispered, "Wow! I'm getting out of here!" He and Dave crawled in the direction of the adjoining apartment building, hopping over the three foot dividing walls. Cautiously approaching an apartment building attached to the stores, they opened a window to the second floor corridor, and began to descend the long staircase that led down to the outside. When halfway down, a cop came rushing up with his head down. Tim knocked him down the stairs with one punch, and jumped over his unconscious body, with Dave on his heels. Off they went with the speed that could only be generated by fear.

I chose to crawl toward the back alley and slide down the gutter. A muscular 'arm of the law' wrapped around my neck from behind, scaring the hell out of me, and with the pistol grip of his gun he hit me on the back of the head, adding, "You're under arrest."

Ignorant of the danger, I bellowed, "Why'd you hit me?" I'm sure that he and the other cops thought they had one of those robbers.

Thank God however, one of the drivers whose car we had bombed, had parked to search for "those little bastards." When he observed the police officer dragging me out from behind the stores, he knew I was one of the culprits. He rushed up, and tried to grab me out of the officer's arms, while shrieking "Let me have that little son of a bitch! I'll show him!"

With my mind focused on this miracle, I whispered, "Thank you God for this man's tenacity!" Thus, instead of being prosecuted for trying to burglarize a store, I was arrested and appeared in the juvenile court system the next day to face a misdemeanor charge.

The judge asked in a threatening tone, "Who were the other two youths with you?"

With my mother standing beside me, I looked straight at him and stated, "We met on the corner that evening. I didn't know them, just a couple of locals who wanted to have some excitement." My poor mother was more scared than I, and showed it, but in her silence she supported me. She knew my stubbornness, the code I would adhere to. Never would I reveal the names of the other two. I would rather go to jail. To my surprise the judge let me go with a slap on the wrist, but he chastised mother. Rather than being elated by the judge's decision, I became angry, saying to him, "My mother is a good mother who does her best. You have no right to criticize her. I'm the one who caused the problem."

The judge seemed surprised to face an angry fifteen year old squirt, 5'6" tall and 115 pounds, who wouldn't allow his mother's feelings to be hurt without a challenge.

The judge's last words, "Well then, respect your mother, and don't cause trouble for her."

"I'll do my best, judge. Thanks!"

Ironically, by the time the three of us had reached 34-35 years of age Tim had become a priest after serving in WW II.

He had returned home disillusioned with life, and decided to join a religious order of priests. David also returned from WW II, continued his formal education on the G.I. Bill, and became a self-employed businessman. I, on the other hand, finished a degree from the University of Illinois, and joined a Catholic Religious Order of Brothers. At 34 I had been working eight years as a missionary on the rugged eastern cost of Nicaragua, committed to teaching the children of the poor.

12

TRAIN RIDES

Each evening a great number of south side business people, who worked in downtown Chicago, would return home on the Rock Island Train to city locations, beginning with 63rd Street, and extending to the south suburbs. In our teen years during WW II, a large number of passenger cars, pulled by an engine and coal car, overflowed with standing passengers.

On the return back to the train yard, only two cars situated in the rear of the train were needed; the unused cars, called 'dark cars', remained unlit and closed to passengers, but they were a tempting invitation to our group to take a free ride.

Any night, it would only take someone to mention, "This is a great night for a train ride. Who's up for it?"

Bill, the first to answer, shouted, "I'm up for it. And you, Joe?"

"Maybe, but we'll be getting back late if we go downtown. Anyway, sure, there's nothing else to do."

The idea floated around, "What do you think, Jack?"

Always ready for one of our usual exploits, Jack answered, "If Frank and Pete will go, I'll go."

I was seldom included in decisions since it was understood I would go if my brother Frank went. Yet, he would always ask me, weighing my input, "You up for a train ride?"

"Of course! I'm always ready for action instead of standing around."

There could be as many as 50 teens gathering on a weekend at 95th and a block from the Suburban Rock Island Line, both Catholic school students and public school students, milling around, talking of the past week's events, sports, school activities, and girls. Those that attended boys' Catholic High Schools with little or no contact with the fair sex, listened to the exploits of the public school guys. They usually had much to say about girls, often greatly exaggerated.

The guys from Catholic schools and public schools had never socialized until we were concerned about a common future, WW II. The youth from Catholic schools were far more risky than the students from public schools, probably because the affluent status of their families provided more security. Frank and I came from 'across the tracks,' where our family struggled during the depression, but the Beverly youth readily accepted Frank, the best athlete and the primary fun-producer at school.

Access to the train was easier for us than a paying passenger; we took the stairs to an empty 'dark cars.' When the train rolled, we sat around in the dark until it moved from ground level to a higher level, about 20 feet above ground. That's when someone would shout, "It's time!" which meant to remove the emergency cords to tie up the handles of the doors. We started with the 'dark car' in front of the occupied passenger cars, providing at least one-car distance ahead of any pursuit. Bulbs were unscrewed and thrown down on the road to explode. The multiple explosions would awaken train personnel to our presence, and the fun would begin.

They had to open the small window of each 'dark car' door from their side to untie the rope, while we kept one car ahead of them. Each car presented the same problem. Whenever they were able to remove cords faster than we were able to utilize them, Frank, the most athletic, would remain behind to entice the first conductor into our strategy of stair-hopping. The other train personnel would return to the passenger cars, and our guys moved faster through the 'dark cars.' Stair-hopping meant one of us would rush down the stairs of one car, and swing out to the stairs of the next car, all the while the train was at full speed. He would continue tantalizing the train- man this way, flying back and forth on the outside of the train, from one set of stairs to the other.

Obviously dangers existed: falling off or being knocked off by some unseen object in the dark, overly close to the train. In fact, on one occasion Pete offered, I'll stay back." He assumed the stair-hopping responsibility, fell off, and broke his arm. On another occasion I was chased up the ladder of the coal car, only to be followed up on top by a conductor. He began to wrestle with me so fiercely that I knew one or both of us would go over the side. Not that crazy, I shouted, "I give up! I give up! You win!"

"Then get going down the ladder!"

"Okay!"

Down at the bottom of the ladder, I kept pushing the conductor's butt back up when he tried to come down, until the train slowed enough for me to jump off.

On another occasion we traveled all the way downtown and walked to a small skid row area on south State Street where we entered a gospel mission. Following fifteen minutes of preaching, the minister shouted out, "How many here are saved?" No one responded. Half were asleep, many were drunk; others were there to get warm.

Our number two Jack, always the clown, inspired by the prolonged silence, responded from the rear, "I am! I'm saved!" The congregation awoke immediately to celebrate the salvation of one of their own, so they thought.

"Come forward young man!" You would think the preacher could recognize a phony, but he was probably happy to get any response from his apathetic congregation.

Jack marched down the aisle at the clapping of the temporary parishioners. The minister hugged him, and said, "Let's go in the back to discuss your salvation." They disappeared far too long and we began to worry.

"Let's check on Jack!" Pete murmured. At that moment the saved-Jack came out shouting again, "I'm saved! I'm saved!"

The parishioners in unison responded in song, "Amen, Amen!"

Nevertheless, in time we found other more exciting activities, and passed this experience to the next generation, but they didn't have our 'smarts', and were inebriated most of the time. One passed out on the tracks and died under the wheels.

13

THE FIRST OPTION TOO OFTEN

One of my nephews, a Marine from Viet Nam days, emailed a story by Retired Major General Chuck Yeager concerning an accidental meeting with Darrell 'Shifty' Powers in the Philadelphia airport. Shifty was returning from France during the yearly trek of WW II vets to the grave sites of their buddies. In the 10 episodes of "Band of Brothers" on the History Channel, 'Shifty' is in every episode. During the conversation with him, the general noticed a 'screaming Eagle' symbol on his hat, and asked, "Where you with the 101st Airborne?"

He answered quietly, "Yes. And after 5 training jumps, my first combat jump was in Normandy. Do you know about that battle?"

"Yes, I know it well."

"I also made a second jump in Holland into the town of Arnhem, one of the most important sites of the Battle of the Bulge."

Suddenly the general recognized a genuine war hero from World War II. Shifty commented, "My visit was sadder than ever because there were so few left, and most of them couldn't make the trip."

Reading this story I wondered how many Americans have knowledge of the Normandy invasion or the Battle of the Bulge! Of the present generation that I asked this question, only one heard of these battles; Normandy, the Allied invasion of the French coast to conquer the Nazis; Arnhem and the Battle of the Bulge, when the Germans, with 20 elite Panzer Divisions, were about to push the Allies back into the sea, if the German tanks could have found fuel.

Shifty commented, "Our vets have nothing like the 'wall' of 59,000 who died in Viet Nam, yet we were considered the Greatest Generation who fought the war to end all wars. I'm told that today school children know more about the Civil War than about WW II."

The thought came to me: How could a ½ million American names from WW II fit on a wall? How could we forget the 60,000,000 people of the world who died in that war? Such a number of deaths are incomprehensible! What stories did our 'leaders' contrive to convince the American people to become a part of the slaughters that followed?

The deaths in the war should have taught us the horrors of war (7 million Polish-18% of their pre-war population; 11 million Chinese; 2 million Japanese; 7 million Germans; 20 million Soviets; over 12 million civilians executed by the Nazis including 6 million Jews; at least one million from a group of smaller countries; and 300,000 - 500,000 Americans.

How could we consider war as a quick solution to conflicts? After WW II the United States became the most powerful country in the world; people in positions of power came to believe that they could exercise that power whenever they wanted. The number of deaths equaled more than 17% of the present population of the United States, or twice the population of California.

"War is a Force That Gives us Meaning," the name of a book written by Chris Hedges, in which he concludes that a country as powerful as ours, with egotistical administrators, will opt for power in solving conflicts. Few will experience the suffering of family or friends; or have the pain and suffering from wars, wars fought by ordinary folk. They find ways to protect their offspring from the military or from dangerous front-line duty in the military.

We invaded Viet Nam with the best of our youth, and remained there 10 years. If the drafted youth, and their families and friends, had not protested in every city, war would have gone on. The youth were not volunteers, but were drafted, enrolled for compulsory service with the armed forces.

The people of power learned from Viet Nam not to have a draft in the future; members of the National Guard were incorporated into the military in Iraq and Afghanistan, and considered as volunteers.

In each invasion or preemptive war in which we participated, I have been saddened, knowing that another generation will die; and those who survived would return home emotionally crippled, disillusioned about life, wander homelessly, or quietly end their own lives. So many friends and former students have perished.

How can we ever find peace if we are always preparing for war?